Place, Race and Politics

How is it that South Sudanese migrants, an overwhelming law-abiding group, have come to be criminalised in Australia? Using the 2016 Moomba 'riot', *Place, Race and Politics* charts the creation of a racialised law and order crisis in Melbourne. This terrific new book provides a detailed analysis of how social and political processes came to associate South Sudanese blackness with violent crime and what the consequences of this criminalisation were on the community. I strongly recommend it.

Karen Farquharson, Professor of Sociology and Vice President of the Academic Board, University of Melbourne

Following in the tradition of Hall et al's classic, *Policing the Crisis, Place Race and Politics: The Anatomy of a Law and Order Crisis* analyses the racialisation and politicisation of crime during the 2018 Victorian election in Australia. Drawn from a number of discrete research projects undertaken by each of the authors, the book is broken down in chapters that largely reflect these different projects. As a result, the authors are able to focus on different elements of the 'law and order crisis' from the demonisation and dangerisation of asylum seekers and immigrant groups, to the media's reportage and amplification of events, the populist political discourse and indeed interviews with those at the coalface of events. It makes for a sobering read as it teases out the long-standing Australian twin political strategies of vilification and law and order auctioneering. As the book shows there are no real winners to come out of such strategies and, ultimately, they serve to undermine the legitimacy even of the political winners – in this case the Victorian Labor party beholden to a tough on crime approach for the foreseeable future. The authors wisely eschew a straight 'moral panic' approach to the topic (while not rejecting it altogether) and offer something more sophisticated. *Race and Politics: The Anatomy of a Law and Order Crisis* makes a significant contribution to critical scholarship on law and order in Australia, but in doing so also explores the tentacles of racism, xenophobia and insecurity that constantly threaten to erode the successful foundations of multi-cultural Australia.

Murray Lee, Professor in Criminology and Associate Dean Research, University of Sydney Law School

Place, Race and Politics: The Anatomy of a Law and Order Crisis

BY

LEANNE WEBER
University of Canberra, Australia

JARRETT BLAUSTEIN
Monash University, Australia

KATHRYN BENIER
Monash University, Australia

REBECCA WICKES
Monash University, Australia

And

DIANA JOHNS
University of Melbourne, Australia

emerald
PUBLISHING

United Kingdom – North America – Japan – India – Malaysia – China

Emerald Publishing Limited
Emerald Publishing, Floor 5, Northspring, 21-23 Wellington Street, Leeds LS1 4DL.

First edition 2021

Reprints and permissions service
Contact: www.copyright.com

British Library Cataloguing in Publication Data
A catalogue record for this book is available from the British Library

ISBN: 978-1-80043-046-4 (Print)
ISBN: 978-1-80043-045-7 (Online)
ISBN: 978-1-80043-047-1 (Epub)
ISBN: 978-1-80043-048-8 (Paperback)

Table of Contents

List of Acronyms

ABC	Australian Broadcasting Corporation
ABS	Australian Bureau of Statistics
ACOSS	Australian Council of Social Services
CBD	Central business district
LNP	Liberal National Party
PSO	Protective Services Officer
UK	United Kingdom
UNHCR	United Nations High Commission for Refugees
US	United States
YNO	Youth network offender

About the Authors

Leanne Weber is a Professor of Criminology at the University of Canberra, Australia, and a Research Associate at the Centre for Criminology, Oxford University. She researches policing and border control using criminological and human rights frameworks. Her books include *Crime, Justice and Human Rights*, 2014 (Palgrave, with Elaine Fishwick and Marinella Marmo); *Policing Non-Citizens*, 2013 (Routledge); *Stop and Search: Police Power in Global Context*, 2013 (Routledge, with Ben Bowling) and *Globalization and Borders: Death at the Global Frontier*, 2011 (Palgrave, with Sharon Pickering), which was awarded the inaugural Christine M Alder Book Prize by the ANZ Society of Criminology.

Jarrett Blaustein is a Senior Lecturer in Criminology in the School of Social Sciences at Monash University. His research currently focusses on intersections between security and sustainable development governance, law and order politics and the global mobility of crime control policies. Jarrett's sole-authored book titled *Speaking Truths to Power: Policy Ethnography and Police Reform in Bosnia and Herzegovina* was nominated by the publisher, Oxford University Press, for the 2016 British Society of Criminology Book Prize and his research also appears in a number of leading criminology journals.

Kathryn Benier is a Lecturer in Criminology in the School of Social Sciences at Monash University. Her research focus is urban criminology and the neighbourhood ecology of crime. Kathryn's work focusses on hate crime and the impact of immigration and ethnic diversity on social relationships, cohesion and sense of belonging over time. Her work primarily investigates the impact of social exclusion and crime on young people, primarily those of African or Muslim heritage. Kathryn has an interest in quantitative methodology and extending new statistical techniques in other fields into criminological research.

Rebecca Wickes is a Professor at the School of Social Sciences at Monash University where she is the Director of the Monash Migration and Inclusion Centre. She is also the Chief Investigator of the Australian Community Capacity Study (ACCS), a multi-million, multi-site, longitudinal study of 298 urban neighbourhoods in Victoria and Queensland. Her research focusses on the spatial concentration of social problems with a particular focus on how physical and demographic changes in urban communities influence social cohesion, the informal regulation of crime and victimisation.

Diana Johns is a Senior Lecturer in Criminology in the School of Social and Political Sciences at the University of Melbourne, where she researches and teaches across the domains of prisons and punishment, children/young people and the criminal legal system and criminal justice knowledge production. Her work is focussed on the effects of criminalisation, the impacts of imprisonment and the possibilities of restorative and relational justice practices. Her book *Being and Becoming an Ex-Prisoner* was published by Routledge in 2018. She is currently working with colleagues on another book, *Coproducing Criminal Justice Knowledge*, to be published by Routledge.

Acknowledgements

The authors acknowledge we are settler occupiers on Aboriginal land. We acknowledge that sovereignty over this land – and by the people of the many Nations who have lived on this Country for thousands of years – has never been ceded.

Collectively, we acknowledge that we live and work on Kulin Country, specifically the land of the Boon Wurrung/Bunurong and Wurundjeri people of the Eastern Kulin nation in and around Melbourne, Victoria, and the land of the Ngunnawal people of the area now known as Canberra and the Ngarigo people of the Snowy Mountains.

We pay respect to Elders, past and present, of all Aboriginal and Torres Strait Islander communities, to their ongoing connection to and care for Country and to the cultural knowledge, wisdom and heritage they hold from the past and carry into the future.

The authors would like to credit Chloe Keel, Greg Koumouris and Claire Moran for their contributions to Chapter 3 and note that they are listed as co-authors of this chapter. Rebecca Powell and Meg Randolph assisted with the collection of data used in the drafting of Chapter 4. We would also like to acknowledge and thank Dr Sara Maher for her advice and assistance in the early developmental stages of the book.

We extend special thanks to Julia Farrell for her expert assistance with editing and compiling the manuscript and for her cheerful forbearance in the face of many delays, the complexities of working with multiple authors and the additional challenges imposed by the very real crisis that is the COVID-19 pandemic.

We would like to restate our thanks to the community members who shared their experiences in our research projects and the community organisations that assisted generously in the recruitment of young people as participants.

The research cited in Chapter 4 would have been impossible without the assistance of the Federation of South Sudanese Associations in Victoria, Afri-Aus Care, Daughters of Jerusalem and local youth and community workers.

The focus groups and interviews discussed in Chapter 5 were conducted with the support of the Centre for Multicultural Youth in Melbourne. We would also like to thank Nyayoud Jice and Barry Berih for their assistance with the project, as well as all of the young people who gave their time.

The interview material included in Chapter 4 was previously published in the following reports:

Weber, L. (2018, December). *'Police are good for some people, but not for us':* *Community perspectives on young people, policing and belonging in Greater* *Dandenong and Casey.* Border Crossing Observatory.
Weber, L. (2020, April). *'You're going to be in the system forever': Policing, risk* *and belonging in Greater Dandenong and Casey.* Border Crossing Observatory.

Some material published in Chapter 5 has been adapted from

Benier, K., Blaustein, J., Johns, D., & Maher, S. (2018). *'Don't drag me into this':* *Growing up South Sudanese in Victoria after the 2016 Moomba 'riot'.* Centre for Multicultural Youth.

In all cases reproduction rights have been retained by the authors.

Chapter 1

Introduction: The Foundations of a Law and Order Crisis

Understanding Law and Order Crises

One Saturday evening in March 2016, the annual Moomba Festival – a whole-of-community event and feature of Melbourne's cultural calendar – was disrupted when violence broke out between a crowd of young people and the police. Despite police reports of feuding groups involving young people from a variety of backgrounds – a multicultural 'melting pot' – the story-hungry media homed in on the so-called Apex gang as the main culprits, and the conflation of 'Apex' and 'Moomba' took hold in the public mind.[1] This gave rise to what scholars and activists often describe as a 'moral panic', which lasted for more than 32 months and then quickly fizzled out in the wake of Victoria's 2018 state election. Media narratives about 'African gangs' and 'Apex thugs' exacted a huge toll on Victoria's African communities and the South Sudanese community in particular.[2] Understanding the processes that fuelled this panic and its consequences requires an examination of the chronology of events; the role of political actors, the police and the media and the nature of the multicultural communities in which this law and order 'crisis' unfolded.

This book presents a multifaceted analysis of the genesis of the 'African gangs' panic by bringing together the findings of multiple empirical research projects conducted, individually and severally, by the book's authors. We were inspired to combine and distil our research data in this way by the pioneering work of Stuart Hall and his colleagues from the Centre for Cultural Studies in Birmingham in *Policing the Crisis: Mugging, the State and Law and Order*, which presented one of the first comprehensive analyses of what they referred to as a 'moral panic' over youth violence that unfolded in the United Kingdom more than four decades ago (Hall et al., 1978). That book charted the creation of a racialised and politicised

---

[1]Assistant Commissioner Leane, of Victoria Police, quoted in Zielinski and Booker (2016).
[2]While the media has often used the generic term 'African' to refer to a wide range of community groups, we use more specific terminology where possible to identify participants in our studies. See Maher et al. (2018) and Wickramaarachchi and Burns (2016) for a discussion of the frequent conflation of groups who identify as Sudanese and South Sudanese in official statistics and discourse.

Place, Race and Politics, 1–21
Copyright © 2021 Leanne Weber, Jarrett Blaustein, Kathryn Benier, Rebecca Wickes and Diana Johns
Published under exclusive licence by Emerald Publishing Limited
doi:10.1108/978-1-80043-045-720211001

media discourse about 'muggings' – a graphic label imported from the United States with no basis in English law – that legitimated a wave of intensive policing directed against a new generation of black British citizens. The book was the first of its kind to bring together the disparate elements of a highly racialised 'moral panic' to produce one explanatory narrative, and possibly the first to introduce systematic media analysis into criminology and identify police and other criminal justice actors as the 'primary definers' of crime (Reiner, 1978).

Policing the Crisis, however, was much more than an analysis of a moral panic. It was ultimately a book about the causes and consequences of racial and material inequality and, specifically, how political and media elites use ideology and culture to construct social problems as criminal threats to reinforce their legitimacy and uphold the status quo. According to Hall et al., the racialised panic over violent crime in the United Kingdom was largely a device to divert attention from a 'crisis of capitalism' and to bolster cross-class consensus in order to smooth the transition to a new, and uncertain, neoliberal order. Their Gramscian analysis – which places processes of political hegemony at its centre – remains influential amongst criminologists today, even though the days of grand theorising on this scale are, for better or worse, behind us.[3]

Hall et al. (1978) embarked on their research as the post-war consensus over welfare provision was beginning to break down in Britain and elsewhere in the world. Within Britain, the radical reforms to the Keynesian welfare state, attacks on the power of labour unions and economic deregulation associated with the policies of Prime Minister Margaret Thatcher unfolded from 1979 to 1990. At the same time, while these transformations to conservative ideology were taking hold and were often perceived as a 'threat to traditional values' (Reiner, 1978, p. 512), a parallel political development was occurring. In a famous speech, which built on the insights provided in *Policing the Crisis*, Stuart Hall (1979) argued that Britain was 'Sleepwalking into a Law and Order Society' characterised by authoritarian populism and an increasing emphasis on the order maintenance role of police.

At the time *Policing the Crisis* was being drafted, Britain had just experienced its first major wave of immigration from former colonies, and a new generation of marginalised 'black British' citizens was emerging (Gilroy, 1987). Emotions about immigration were running high, notwithstanding the fact that, as renowned UK anti-racist activist Ambalavaner Sivanandan noted in relation to postcolonial migration, 'We are here, because you were there' (cited in Younge, 2018), emotions about immigration were running high. This set the scene for authoritarian populism to take on a particularly racialised character. While multiculturalism was never explicitly mentioned as a historical 'conjuncture' underpinning the hegemonic crisis posited in Hall et al.'s book, and matters of race were considered by those authors to be mediated through class, one contemporary commentator has noted that the book was nevertheless 'centrally framed by and through race' (Murji, 2020, p. 450).

Fast-forward to the first two decades of the twenty-first century, neoliberalism has become near-hegemonic on a global scale, ushering in a sustained period of

---

[3]See Fatsis (2021) for a contemporary assessment of the book's legacy.

structural insecurity for working people across both the developed and less-developed world characterised by the deliberate creation of job insecurity and the transfer of government resources from service provision towards policies of exclusion and law enforcement. In many respects, the 'drift' identified by Stuart Hall (1979) has gained pace and the 'law and order society' he predicted seems to now be much closer on the horizon. At the same time, global economic inequality and political instability have given rise to widespread population movements, bringing with them a nationalist backlash in which anti-immigrant sentiments have gained political purchase, even in countries, such as Australia, with long-standing commitments to multiculturalism. If *Policing the Crisis* was written against a backdrop of a 'crisis of capitalism', then our book is written in a context where a pervasive 'contestation over membership' concerning some groups of immigrants is also a determining feature (Bosworth & Guild, 2008; Franko, 2020).

Although the contexts – in both a historical and a geographical sense – are somewhat distinct, we believe there are important continuities and similarities in terms of process between the construction of Melbourne's 'African gangs crisis' and Britain's 'mugging crisis'. Thus, while this book is less ambitious in its scope than the classic work that inspired it, it nevertheless tells a story about how politics, policing and journalism actively contributed to the construction of a racialised 'folk devil' in Melbourne at a particular point in time. This, in turn, prompts consideration of the wider social impacts of the sustained demonisation of African Australians in terms of community attitudes and social cohesion, and the politics of race and crime, in a relatively prosperous, progressive and diverse late capitalist society.

While there are important parallels between this book and *Policing the Crisis*, it is not our intention to present an updated version of that classic text. Nor do we seek to use our more recent example as an opportunity to assess the 'validity' of Hall et al.'s theoretical claims about the deployment of a 'moral panic' by political elites to shore up hegemony.[4] Rather, our analysis of the 'African gangs crisis' draws more loosely on Hall et al.'s rich, holistic, place-based and histori-cised account of the 'mugging crisis', which sheds light on how the criminalisation of a racialised folk devil is shaped by an interplay of cultural, political and structural forces. While *Policing the Crisis* has been described as a book of two parts – an empirically informed analysis that examines institutional processes, combined with an ideologically driven and explanatory structural analysis – we focus primarily on the former, treating wider social and economic forces largely as 'background' (Horton, 1979). In contrast to Hall et al.'s predominantly 'top-down' approach, our discussion also includes original research that reflects the experiences of affected communities. This avoids the criticism levelled at those authors of 'eschew[ing] empirical lived reality … in pursuit of deeper structures' (McMullan & Ratner, 1982, p. 236). And while *Policing the Crisis* has attracted

---

[4]For critiques of the overall success of this endeavour, see McMullan and Ratner (1982), Schlesinger (1979) and Turk (1980).

criticism in some quarters for treating race and racism largely as a 'footnote' (Horton, 1979; but see Fatsis, 2021, for an alternative view), we position race and other markers of non-belonging at the front and centre of our analysis in recognition of the openly racialised labelling that has characterised the 'African gangs' phenomenon.

Theorising Risk, Security and Othering

While *Policing the Crisis* provides a natural anchor point for our work, we also avail ourselves of the considerable volume of academic literature that has accrued on a range of topics since the publication of this classic text. In response to social, political and economic changes around the world, new analytical frameworks have emerged to deal with the rapid transformations taking place under globalisation and the consolidation of both neoliberalism and authoritarianism.

For one thing, the concept of 'moral panic' has been subjected to sustained critique and refinement (Cornwell & Linders, 2002; Hier, 2008; Horsley, 2017). Even though *Policing the Crisis* integrated observations from multiple cultural, economic and political domains, over time the terminology of 'moral panic' has come to be seen as reductionist and incapable of explaining the multiple processes that combine to produce these phenomena. Subsequent research has also served to illuminate the complex political and cultural processes that contribute to 'moral panics', directly and indirectly and intentionally and unintentionally. We reflect on some of these processes in Chapters 2 and 3; however, it is not our desire to rehash these debates or discuss the validity of moral panic theory today. Rather, mindful of this historical critique, we adopt the more contemporary terminology of 'law and order crisis' to describe the construction of the 'African gangs' threat. This terminology has emerged as an analytical tool of choice across many fields of policy analysis. For example, Wonders and Cerys (forthcoming) note that nation-states around the world are increasingly framing governance challenges such as the control of spontaneous border crossing in terms of 'crisis', in order to justify harsh border controls, the application of executive power and other repressive measures that short-circuit democratic accountability (see also Koulish & van der Woude, 2020; McAdam, 2013; Tazreiter, 2018).

The concept of crisis is underpinned by heightened perceptions of risk, both in general and through the association of risk with particular places, events or people. The allocation of specific individuals or groups of people to risk categories has often been a precursor to their differential treatment, including increased surveillance or exclusionary measures directed towards 'high-risk' people (Armstrong, 2004; Harcourt, 2015; O'Malley, 1994; Pratt, 2017; Pratt et al., 2005). The concept of risk, therefore, is also part of our theoretical repertoire. Understood as the calculation of the probability of harm, risk is often seen as the predominant organising principle for crime control and other areas of governance under neoliberalism. Risk theorists have described the style of governance they associate with heightened risk perceptions and individualistic neoliberal ideology as 'governing through crime' (Simon, 2007).

This mode of neoliberal governance and the underlying ideological and economic conditions that have given rise to it have come to be associated with the phenomenon of penal populism in Anglophone democracies, which is characterised by a preference for punitive responses to social problems rather than a welfare-based approach (discussed in Chapter 2). In the context of growing socioeconomic inequality, increasingly punitive penal policies and practices effectively serve to punish marginalised communities (Wacquant, 2009). Reflecting on these transformations and their impact on state penality, Bauman (2013, pp. 43–44) writes:

> The protective functions of the state are tapered and 'targeted', to embrace a small minority of the unemployable and the invalid, though even that minority tends to be reclassified step by step from an object of social care into an issue of law and order; the incapacity of an individual to engage in the market game according to its statutory rules while using their own resources and at their own personal risk tends to be increasingly criminalized or suspected of criminal intention, or at any rate criminal potential.

Closely associated with risk is a preoccupation with security, the state of being free from danger or risk of harm, which is increasingly applied at the individual and community level, as well as the national level (Zedner, 2009). The cognate process of securitisation refers to a condition in which social issues are framed almost exclusively in terms of the pursuit of security (Bigo, 2011; Rose, 1999), often displacing other values such as due process or fairness. Critical scholars have argued that the categorisation of people according to risk categories – whether formal or informal – can lead to the security of marginalised groups being sacrificed in pursuit of security and wellbeing for the majority, with counter-terrorism being a frequently cited example (McCulloch & Wilson, 2016; Zedner, 2010). More recently, this idea has been adapted in the field of border criminology, with 'governing through immigration control' being presented as a method for bolstering perceptions of security for citizens, while also reinforcing the boundaries of membership and inclusion, often in highly racialised ways (Bosworth & Guild, 2008).

A considerable body of scholarship has also advanced our understanding of processes of racialisation (Cunneen, 2020; Das Gupta et al., 2007; Hervik, 2019; Parmar et al., 2020). This term is underpinned by a belief in the socially constructed nature of 'race'. It refers to the process by which particular groups come to be collectively identified through physical characteristics, such as skin colour, that are popularly associated with race and can also be applied more broadly to the ways in which social institutions become 'imbued with racial meanings' (Murji, 2006, p. 334).

In Australia, as in other places, risk has imbued youth justice as an ordering concept for over two decades, during which time it has become increasingly fused with race and indigeneity. Risk assessment in youth justice involves tools that are 'apparently neutral and non-discriminatory', but which are, in practice, highly racialised (Cunneen, 2020). Cunneen argues that risk assessment, as an 'evidence-based' and therefore 'scientised' practice, both *masks* race and *marks* black and Indigenous youth as 'risky'. When risk is put to work as a concept to stand in for dangerousness, it carries this mask and these marks with it. Indicators of imputed 'dangerousness' are validated and legitimised through a 'risk' lens that categorises and classifies, measures and objectifies. Through this lens, danger becomes knowable and can be factored into institutional logics for maintaining order, ensuring safety and managing security. But because, as Cunneen (2020) argues, risk is racialised, so then is dangerousness.

Here, the concept of *dangerisation* is useful for understanding how certain racial categories, youth and crime are conflated and thus come to be perceived as threats to order and safety. Dangerisation, according to Lianos and Douglas (2000, p. 267),

> ...is the tendency to perceive and analyse the world through categories of menace ... to continuously scan and assess public and private spaces in terms of potential threats by other people.

They explain that when 'democratic, civil society imposes its highly institutionalised, formally egalitarian model of social coexistence, difference and otherness can only be established in terms of dangerousness' (2000, p. 267). From this perspective, in places that celebrate multiculturalism and diversity on the one hand, and a safe and tolerant community on the other, citizens

> ...build their old lines of bias on the new legitimizing basis of danger ... presumed dangerousness is the major postindustrial criterion for distinguishing between those who should be avoided and those who can approach.
>
> (2000, pp. 267–268)

When we consider how securitisation sacrifices the safety of some for the security of the majority (Zedner, 2010), dangerisation can be seen as both activator and amplifier of securitising processes, and making this connection helps explain how the safety of racialised young people may be sacrificed ostensibly for the safety and security of the wider community.

Dangerisation is not recognised as a matter of racial discrimination, however, because it is coded as community safety, public order and individual security. In this way race is 'laundered' through risk (Goddard & Myers, 2017) and rendered 'colourblind' (Gonzalez Van Cleve & Mayes, 2015). For middle-class progressives, this is palatable, tolerable and, indeed, entirely reasonable. For lawmakers and law-enforcers, according to Lianos and Douglas (2000, p. 269), the 'projection of menace ... at a large scale ... becomes a contemporary way of building institutional legitimacy'. This arises in the identification and perceived quelling of potential danger, as they qualify: 'Dangerization does not ascertain the *existence* of dangers. It is rather a constant skill of scanning the environment for perceptual indices of irregularity, which are then perceived as menacing' (Lianos & Douglas, 2000, p. 273).

This process is nothing new. As early as the 1960s, US policing scholar Jerome Skolnick argued that the 'underlying collectively held sentiments, which justify penal sanctions, arise ultimately and most clearly from the threat of violence and the possibility of danger to the community' (Skolnick, 1966, p. 45). This scanning for danger could lead, he argued, to the identification by police of 'symbolic assailants' as a kind of 'perceptual shorthand', mediated by a range of factors including appearance and demeanour, but often attached to race. While there may indeed be high levels of offending associated with certain groups at times, Skolnick (2007, p. 69) warned of a 'ratchet effect' that 'occurs when racial profiling produces a supervised population disproportionate to the distribution of offending by the racial group'. 'Danger-based legitimacy' (Lianos & Douglas, 2000, p. 269), then, is garnered through strategies of control directed at people or groups deemed 'risky'.

These risk-reduction strategies targeting non-citizens are consistent with the intense contestation over membership that has arisen under the destabilising conditions of globalisation. This contestation embeds immigration status, as well as race, into processes of dangerisation. Katja Franko (2020, p. 3) has described the production of 'crimmigrant others' in Europe as a process in which particular groups of unwanted migrants come to be associated with criminality and seen as a wider threat to an increasingly fragile moral order:

> Immigrants are no longer people in need of protection, or a potential source of labour; they have been turned into rule-breakers and criminal offenders, or what can be termed "crimmigrant others." Their presence is associated with illegality and crime.

There is no suggestion that this label is explicitly applied by politicians, state agents or members of the public. Rather, crimmigrant others may come to be recognised in the popular imagination as 'queue jumpers' or 'people smugglers' or members of 'African gangs'. While some individual migrants do become law-breakers, Franko notes the malleability of this label so that crimmigrants may be so classified as a group, more on the basis of their perceived difference and non-belonging than due to their actual criminality. Indeed, we might contend that it may not even be necessary to be an immigrant in order to be considered a crimmigrant; for example, where young people born or raised in the country of residence, but whose parents were born elsewhere, are continually reminded of their outsider status. Dangerisation describes the process whereby difference comes to be seen in terms of danger and strategies of control through the lens of risk.

Like Lianos and Douglas, Franko (2020) sees the putative labelling of certain migrants as crimmigrants as a legitimating device, transforming them into targets of 'penal power' and 'justified social exclusion'. Crimmigrants may be subjected to intensive surveillance, punishment or deportation, while at the same time governments can claim a continuing commitment to multiculturalism and universal human rights, thus creating a 'paradox of social exclusion' in a 'seemingly inclusive society' (p. 111), a paradox also explained by Lianos and Douglas (2000; Lianos, 2013). Just as, according to Hall et al., the casting of black British youths as dangerous offenders diverted attention from the conditions of social and economic marginalisation to which they were exposed, Franko sees the exclusion of the 'crimmigrant other' as a device to shore up a deeply unequal global order.

> Through the control of the crimmigrant other, contemporary modalities of penal power are a central mechanism for guarding the boundaries of citizenship. They mobilise notions of innocence, goodness, right, and wrong in the processes of the making and unmaking of contemporary membership and belonging. The growing use of penal power at the border speaks of the increasingly contentious and privileged nature of Northern citizenship and residence rights in a deeply unequal global order.
>
> (2020, p. 198)

In Australia, as elsewhere, immigration policy has generated racist, criminalising 'us and them' tropes that have shaped exclusionary punitive discourse and ideas about 'the good society'. These narratives have hinged on otherness as a category of menace that has somehow enabled a collective apathy and acceptance of increasingly punitive practices cloaked in legitimising justifications (Windle, 2008). This is an example of how, as Lianos (2013, p. 2) asserts, 'otherness can easily and unjustifiably be associated with dangerousness, but it can also arbitrarily be manipulated as a social force through dangerousness'. This explains 'the direct but unfounded link between insecurity and poor ethnic minorities' and how 'African youth' came to represent danger, menace and a threat to order and security within both conservative authoritarian logic and 'progressive' forms of social control.

Understanding the Moomba 'Riot'

Although the process associating African migrants with crime was set in motion many years earlier, the emergence of the 'African gangs' label in the public arena coincided with the Moomba Festival in 2016. This is a longstanding and unique community event described as a family-friendly celebration of the city's diversity and talent. Organised annually by the City of Melbourne since 1955, the Moomba Festival attracts more than one million people to the city's central business district (CBD). On the Saturday evening, 12 March 2016, Moomba crowds gathered along the Yarra River in Melbourne's CBD in anticipation of a fireworks show. Just before 8 p.m., a fight broke out in Federation Square. It is not entirely clear what sparked the incident but reports would later suggest that a group of white men racially abused a group of young men from African backgrounds who were walking past and this triggered one of three separate fights (Hosking, 2016). These fights were described by journalists as a 'series of affrays' (Calligeros, 2016) and a 'rolling brawl' (Mills & Houston, 2016) involving up to 150 people (Zielinski &

Booker, 2016). According to one security consultant (quoted in Woods, 2017b) who had been contracted for the event, fights were a regular feature of the Moomba Festival: 'Every year there's always issues … There's always gangs, there's always fights, it's just what happens … So this year wasn't … anything out of the ordinary'.

Whatever previous fights may have occurred at Moomba, other public celebrations in Melbourne's CBD did not attract significant media coverage nor did they give rise to full-blown law and order crises. What, then, was different about the 2016 'affrays' that came to be labelled a 'riot'?

Was the scale of the disorder at Moomba in 2016 greater than it had been in previous years? This is actually difficult to assess because previous incidents of a similar nature that had allegedly occurred during Moomba attracted no significant media attention and were therefore poorly documented. The only comparable incident (as reported in the media) in the five years preceding the disorder at Moomba that did seemingly resonate is said to have occurred during the 2013–2014 New Year's Eve celebrations in Melbourne's CBD. An article published in *The Sunday Age* cited claims by 'community workers' that 'police played down a violent New Year's brawl between more than 200 youths of African appearance … for fear of being accused of racism' (Stark, 2014). The nature and scale of the disorder, the location and the article's description of the alleged perpetrators, which emphasised their 'African' heritage, all appear to be consistent with how the disorder at Moomba was reported, but the incident failed to attract wider coverage or generate a political buzz. In fact, the only other coverage that this 2013–2014 incident received from Melbourne's print media was a blog post penned by a controversial ultra-conservative media commentator named Andrew Bolt, who accused police and reporters of covering up the incident due to concerns about political correctness (Bolt, 2014). Bolt, who has built his career on fanning the flames of the culture wars, is a recurring character in our story and elements of his consistently and explicitly racialised narrative would later influence the dominant conservative framing of the 'African gangs crisis'.[5]

A further point to consider is that the immense cultural and political significance attached to the disorder at Moomba was, at least in our view, vastly disproportionate to the actual scale of what reportedly occurred that night. Compared to the 2011 England riots, which unfolded over four nights, affected multiple cities, 'resulted in five deaths, injuries to dozens of police officers and civilians and damage to and loss of property running into the tens of millions of pounds' (Newburn, 2015, p. 39), the disorder at Moomba was trivial. It lasted a few hours, involved a few hundred people at most and resulted in no serious injuries or significant property damage. As discussed in Chapter 2, however, Moomba was not trivial from a political standpoint. In this regard, the legacy of the incident in relation to policy (albeit perhaps not from a cultural standpoint)

---

[5]Bolt's contrarian and seemingly intentionally provocative views are afforded a platform in Rupert Murdoch–owned media outlets (Sky News and the *Herald Sun*). For non-Australian readers, his role and status as a media figure is seemingly comparable to Tucker Carlson in the United States.

had arguably more impact than the 2011 England riots (Newburn et al., 2018). Disproportionality is also evident in relation to the coverage of subsequent criminal incidents, including carjackings and home invasions that were attributed to Australians of South Sudanese heritage. For both the 'African gangs crisis' and England's 'mugging crisis' of the 1970s, it was seemingly the racialised characteristics of the 'folk devils' that rendered their crimes newsworthy rather than the crimes themselves.

Another compelling explanation relates to the imagery of the disorder, the accessibility of this imagery to journalists and its cultural significance. Importantly, in the first instance, the disorder at Moomba was caught on camera: CCTV and mobile phone footage captured young people running, brawling, shouting and being capsicum-sprayed by police (Woods, 2017b). The photographs that appeared in Australian newspapers and were circulated on social media overwhelmingly depicted familiar imagery: a conflict between young black men or teenagers wearing street clothes and white police officers. It is therefore unsurprising that young people from migrant backgrounds, specifically those of South Sudanese heritage, quickly came to be associated with gang activity and were overwhelmingly presented as the antagonists and instigators of this disorder. Indeed, the racialised connotations of the 'gang' label and its political utility as a vehicle for dangerisation are widely noted by criminologists (Hallsworth & Young, 2008).

Interestingly, police were not represented in the media as the protagonists of the incident, but rather, they faced criticism for their perceived inability or unwillingness to anticipate and contain the disorder (Houston et al., 2016). In typical fashion, the following day Andrew Bolt claimed that the disorder at Moomba was not only symptomatic of a larger longstanding problem with 'refugees' and 'African gangs', but also that centre-left Labor politicians in Victoria along with multiple Chief Commissioners and journalists had refused to acknowledge this (Bolt, 2016). Underpinning Bolt's framing of the 'African gang' problem as a non-white immigration problem was an enduring conservative critique of multiculturalism that is rooted in Australia's colonial past and racist 'White Australia' ideology (Jayasuriya, 2003).[6] The victims of the disorder at Moomba were then depicted as the entire community, represented by the festival goers, bystanders and local business owners who were said to be harmed by the incident.

Returning to our point about imagery, arguably the most iconic and influential photograph from the evening depicted a small team of white police officers deploying capsicum spray to disperse a group of young black men in Federation Square. This image, which was published in the *Herald Sun* (Victoria's most widely circulated newspaper), undoubtedly helped to shape the public's understanding of the event by supplying visual evidence that appeared to support the dominant narrative of conflict between unruly African migrants and police as the protectors of a prosperous, diverse and tolerant society. This is an example of

---

[6]The title of the blog post includes the question, 'Why did we import this danger?'

the intimate union of media and political narratives in the dangerisation process. Less influential from a cultural standpoint, however, was a video documenting the events leading up to this incident from the perspective of a member of the crowd, which was uploaded to YouTube the following day by a local radio station (3AW, 2016). The video, which only attracted a few thousand views, depicts what appears to be an ethnically diverse crowd of young people encircling a small number of police officers while chanting 'fuck the police' in the seconds leading up to the deployment of capsicum spray. The apparent diversity of the crowd raises questions about the validity of the dominant narrative that attributed blame to 'Sudanese gangs', and it is unclear who or what exactly triggered the escalation in the police response.

Regardless of what actually transpired that night, the disorder at Moomba became the subject of highly racialised and enduring media coverage that singled out young people from South Sudanese and other African backgrounds. Media coverage of 'African youth', 'gangs' and 'Sudanese' increased exponentially following the Moomba event, and it persisted until November 2018 when the conservative Liberal–National Coalition lost the state election on a law and order platform. A more detailed analysis of the ebbs and flows of media coverage is provided in Chapter 3, but despite attempts by some senior police and many community leaders, South Sudanese Australian and otherwise, to add nuance and perspective to the discussion, a reductionist narrative remained dominant during this 32-month period.

The South Sudanese Diaspora in Melbourne

Located in the state of Victoria, Melbourne was designated 'the world's most liveable city' by *The Economist* (2016) for six straight years (2011–2016). This designation has been a source of pride for many Melburnians and reflects the city's economic prosperity, local environment, cultural and sporting offerings and public. Like any city, however, Melbourne and its surrounding suburbs have social and economic problems, with evidence of increasing segregation on the basis of income and ethnicity. Sydes and Wickes's (2021) recent research reveals that Indigenous Australians and those who speak a language other than English are not only living in the poorest neighbourhoods but are also absent in higher socioeconomic areas. Additionally, income inequality and unemployment levels are significantly higher for first-generation migrants to Australia born in non-English-speaking countries (8.5%) compared to the Australian-born population (4.6% – Australian Bureau of Statistics (ABS), 2011). For members of Victoria's South Sudanese community, the unemployment rate in the lead-up to the Moomba 'riot' was significantly higher again, at 23% (Markus, 2015, p. 4).

Sudanese/South Sudanese Australians are one of the country's largest 'new' communities from a refugee background (see, for example, Robinson, 2013) and possibly the largest diaspora group in the world. Migrants from Sudan and South Sudan predominantly arrived in Australia through the humanitarian visa programme between 2001 and 2006, during the Sudanese civil war (Maher et al.,

2018; Refugee Council, 2018). During this period, approximately 2,200 ethnic Sudanese, born to Sudanese parents in refugee camps in Egypt or Kenya, also immigrated to Australia (Stevenson, 2009). According to the 2016 ABS Census, approximately 25,000 Sudanese/South Sudanese people live in Australia, largely in major Australian cities (90%): Melbourne (31%); Sydney (22%); Perth (13%) and Brisbane (12%).

Looking at the figures in Tables 1.1 and 1.2, it is clear that not only is the Sudanese/South Sudanese community experiencing greater levels of unemployment, but ialso they are concentrated in non-professional occupations (ABS, 2016).

This economic and social inequality is also generational such that young people (aged 25–34) are earning less income (adjusted for inflation and rising cost of living) and own fewer assets than previous generations (ACOSS, 2015).

This over-/under-representation is partially explained by the heightened levels of social exclusion, relative poverty and educational barriers generally experienced by resettled refugee communities in Australia (Taylor, 2004). Of equal note is the level of discrimination against members of the Sudanese/South Sudanese community. There is significant evidence that the Sudanese/South Sudanese community has struggled with 'acculturation stress' arising from family breakdown, historical trauma, the complexity of transnational identities, ongoing ethnic and political divisions within the diaspora and widespread experiences of racism and exclusion in their new environment (Maher et al., 2018). Indeed, 77% of the South Sudanese

Table 1.1. Employment Status for Sudanese/South Sudanese as at the 2016 ABS Census.

	Sudanese/South Sudanese in Melbourne	Overall Melbourne Population	Overall Australian Population
Employed, worked full-time	18%	38%	37%
Employed, worked part-time	15%	20%	20%
Employed, away from work	5%	3%	3%
Unemployed, looking for full-time work	11%	2%	3%
Unemployed, looking for part-time work	7%	2%	2%
Not in the labour force	45%	34%	35%
Total	100%	100%	100%

Table 1.2. Industry of Employment for Sudanese/South Sudanese as at the 2016 ABS Census.

	Sudanese/South Sudanese in Melbourne	Overall Melbourne Population	Overall Australian Population
Managers	4%	13%	13%
Professionals	12%	25%	23%
Technicians and trades workers	6%	13%	14%
Community and personal service workers	30%	10%	11%
Clerical and administrative workers	7%	14%	14%
Sales workers	8%	10%	10%
Machinery operators and drivers	13%	6%	6%
Labourers	20%	8%	10%
Total	100%	100%	100%

participants in the 2015 Scanlon Foundation Survey reportedly experienced racism in the 12 months prior (Markus, 2015, p. 60). This was the highest of any group surveyed.

Contextualising Moomba and the 'African Gangs Crisis'

Racial discrimination against African Australians in Victoria is also particularly well-documented in the criminal justice sphere. For example, a 2007 study conducted by the Refugee Health Research Centre found that more than 50% of young male refugees in Melbourne had been stopped and questioned by police (Refugee Health Research Centre, 2007, cited in Windle, 2008, p. 556). The nature of this discrimination can be inferred from scholarly articles and non-government organisation reports that document the over-policing of South Sudanese refugees and other African Australians by Victorian police since the mid-2000s (see, for example, Australian Human Rights Commission, 2010; Run, 2013; Smith & Reside, 2010).

Historically, the over-policing of African Australian youth has been associated with their visible presence in public spaces. Conflicting views held by African Australian young people and the police about the legitimate use of public space have therefore been identified as an important source of conflict between these two groups (Smith & Reside, 2010). A consequence is that African Australian youth regularly feel unwelcome in public spaces because of their ethnicity (Smith & Reside, 2010). It is worth noting that, following a 2012 parliamentary review of police use of 'stop-and-search' powers (Victorian Government, 2012), Victoria Police has attempted to address these discriminatory practices and improve its relations with African Australian communities, albeit with questionable success. These efforts were redoubled after the *Haile-Michael* litigation brought under the Commonwealth *Racial Discrimination Act 1975* – which was decided in the Federal Court in 2013 via a settlement with Victoria Police – established that the African Australian complainants had been subjected to discriminatory policing through repeated and unjustified street stops.[7] In 2014, for example, Victoria Police established a Priority Communities Division and implemented anti-racial profiling policies, including training on bias for all new recruits, data monitoring and a 'stop-and-search' receipting pilot that was ultimately unsuccessful (Victoria Police, 2021). The impact of these initiatives on police–community relations in the lead-up to Moomba was seemingly limited, however, given that 59% of South Sudanese participants in the 2015 Scanlon Foundation Survey indicated that they had experienced discrimination from the police specifically in the past year (Markus, 2015, p. 60).

It is also important to acknowledge that Australian politicians and media outlets have long played a role in constructing and perpetuating problematic racialised narratives about migrant communities and their youth. The South Sudanese community was first subjected to this during a series of interviews and press conferences that took place in October 2007, when (then) Federal Immigration Minister Kevin Andrews cited concerns over South Sudanese 'gangs' in Victoria and what he described as their difficulty in 'settling and adjusting', as a justification for reducing the intake of African refugees (Due, 2008; Farouque et al., 2007). These comments, quickly labelled racist by members of the Labor Opposition, were largely consistent with commonly used descriptions of African Australian youth by the conservative media in the aftermath of violent incidents. To this effect, Windle (2008) has argued that groups of young men from the African Australian community are frequently described by the media as 'mobs', 'packs', 'gangs' and 'thugs', thereby reinforcing the idea that this is a problem population (Windle, 2008, p. 558). For example, one such article was published in the popular Victorian tabloid the *Herald Sun* eight months prior to Minister Andrews's comments with the headline, 'Lock out these refugee thugs' (Wright, 2007). This suggests that racialised and xenophobic narratives concerning 'African gangs' circa 2016 were not novel, but rather latent in the years preceding Moomba.

Interestingly, prevailing racialised narratives about the South Sudanese community did not factor into either the 2010 or the 2014 Victorian state elections. In 2010, a Liberal–National Coalition narrowly defeated the incumbent Labor Party

---

[7]*Haile-Michael v Konstantinidis* [2012] FCA 108, [2012] FCA 167, [2013] FCA 53.

on a platform that included 'law and order' issues such as the abolition of suspended sentences for serious offences, violence on public transport, regulating the night-time economy, and a recent wave of attacks on Indian students (Rood, 2010). It is worth noting that the Liberals were the 'primary definers' (to use Hall et al.'s terminology) of this 'law and order' agenda but both parties adopted 'tough on crime' platforms in an effort to appeal to voters.[8] 'Law and order' politics appeared to have had a negligible impact on the 2014 election when the Labor Opposition, led by Daniel Andrews, defeated the Coalition government on a platform that called for investment in public infrastructure, job creation and protecting the environment.

Despite an increase in the youth *reoffending* rate in Victoria during the four-year period leading up to the Moomba 'riot', overall youth offending had been steadily declining (Millsteed & Sutherland, 2016) and crime was not a major political issue at the time of this event. This is evident from a March 2016 poll, which found that most Victorians did not consider crime to be one of the three most important issues in the state (IPSOS, 2016, p. 3; see Fig. 1.1).

It is also evidenced by the fact that the leader of the Liberal Opposition, Matthew Guy, did not publish a single tweet about crime during the two months immediately prior to the Moomba Festival.[9] By comparison, several of his tweets during the two-year period following the Moomba 'riot' focussed on various aspects of this issue in an effort to portray the Andrews government as weak and ineffective on crime.

Contextualising the 2016 Moomba 'riot' also necessitates consideration of previous episodes of public disorder that took place in Melbourne. We have already noted reports of similar disorder that was alleged to have occurred during the 2013–2014 New Year's celebrations, but the most significant event in recent memory was the protest against the Group of 20 (G20) global economic summit that took place in Melbourne in November 2006. The Australian Broadcasting Corporation (ABC) described the disorder as follows:

> A protest against the G20 Summit in Melbourne has turned violent with some members of the crowd kicking police horses and throwing eggs at officers. About 2,000 chanting protesters have marched through Melbourne towards the venue of the G20. A police van has been destroyed and barricade lines broken as the protest turns ugly. Protesters have thrown glass bottles, flares and steel rods at police, and upturned barricades were also hurled at police in riot gear....

---

[8]For non-Australian readers, it is important to note that Liberal parties in Australia at both the state and federal levels are clearly positioned to the right of centre and contain some far-right elements.

[9]https://twitter.com/search?f=tweets&vertical=default&q=from%3AMatthewGuyMP%20since%3A2016-01-01%20until%3A2016-03-12&src=typd&lang=en.

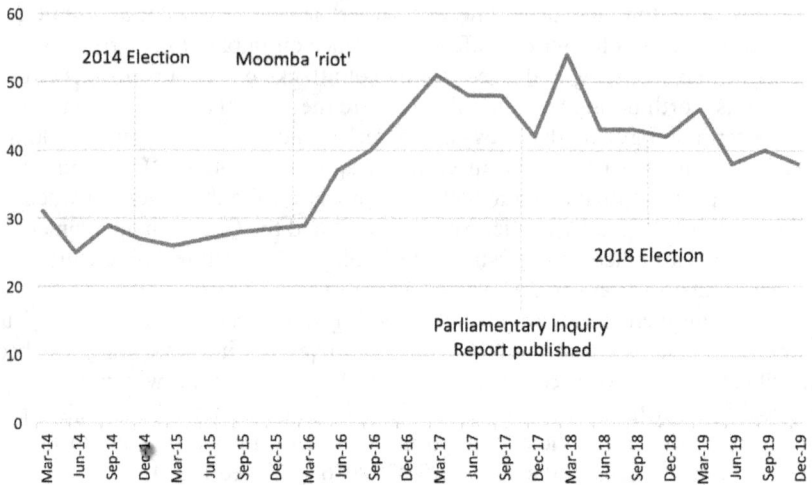

Fig. 1.1.   Percentage of Victorians Who Identified 'Crime' as One of
the Three Most Important Issues in Victoria.
Source: IPSOS Issues Monitors (2015–2019).[10]

The scale of this disorder was significantly greater than what occurred at Moomba but, more significantly, it was overtly political in nature.

There were, however, two other reports of large 'brawls' between groups of young people in Melbourne that were subsequently characterised by the media in racialised terms (that is, describing the youths as African, Pasifika and Asian – see Dowsley, 2009; Stark, 2014; Xureb & Evans, 2007). These incidents (2007, 2009) reportedly occurred at a shopping centre in the western suburbs of Melbourne and attracted relatively limited media attention. Despite their similarities to the disorder at Moomba, these incidents (like the New Year's Eve disorder) did not attract the 'riot' label, political attention, or have significant implications for criminal justice policy in Victoria.

The 'riot' label was applied, however, to a series of incidents that occurred at youth justice facilities in Victoria in the lead-up to the 2016 Moomba 'riot' (Victorian Ombudsman, 2017). One such incident occurred just one week prior to the Moomba Festival, when Victoria Police's Public Order Response Team was called to the Parkville Youth Justice Precinct where six 'out-of-control teenage inmates' had climbed onto the roof of the building and, armed with sticks and poles, were 'smashing windows and skylights and tearing apart a chimney and air-conditioning units' and screaming and shouting at police (Hamblin & Cavanagh, 2016). Images published by the media suggest that the participants were from diverse ethnic backgrounds, but the significant media coverage of this incident illustrates that the 'riot' label was in circulation at the time of the Moomba Festival.

---

[10]https://www.ipsos.com/en-au/ipsos-issues-monitor.

Finally, it is worth considering that the framing of the incident at Moomba was likely influenced, at least indirectly, by narratives about the 2011 England riots that circulated in the Australian media. For starters, we note that the disorder in England attracted significant media attention in Australia and likely served as an important cultural reference point for making sense of what occurred at Moomba (questions of comparability aside). More directly, however, the England riots seemingly fuelled concerns among police and community groups that something similar could happen in Melbourne. Articles highlighting this possibility were published in both the conservative *Herald Sun* and later in the centre-progressive newspaper *The Age*. What is perhaps most interesting about this coverage is how the perceived risk of something similar occurring was represented in the different papers. In the *Herald Sun*, the problem was presented as youth gangs

> ...linked to assaults, stabbings and brawls, a Molotov cocktail attack on a train, the firebombing of a home and attacks with deadly weapons including machetes, tomahawks, tasers, bars, baseball bats, bottles and knuckle-dusters.
>
> (Mickelburough, 2011)

By contrast, an article that appeared in *The Age* framed the problem as one of social exclusion and racism that was exemplified by the ongoing over-policing of African Australians. Elements of both problematisations would resonate with elements of the subsequent coverage of the Moomba riot.

Arguably the most inflammatory take on the England riots by an Australian commentator was penned by Andrew Bolt, who criticised the media for what he described as their unwillingness to 'report some hard truths about the rioters, not least the predominant race of the first troublemakers':

> True, there were many "other white guys" among the rioters, but only a coward or a fool would ignore the racial dimension and the immigration failures that led to the initial violence, allegedly set off when a black hood was fatally shot by police.
>
> (Bolt, 2011)

Bolt's attempt to locate the cause of the disorder in England with the failure, inability and/or unwillingness of black migrants to integrate into British society is again consistent with elements of the dominant construction of the 'African gangs crisis' in the conservative press almost five years later. In essence, this narrative locates responsibility for criminality with marginalised communities and the so-called politically correct institutions that fail to control them.

A narrative of marginalisation directed against the South Sudanese Australian community can be traced from at least 2007, when a young South Sudanese Australian man, Liep Gony, was murdered in a racist attack by two white men in south-east Melbourne. The response of Federal Immigration Minister Kevin Andrews was to voice concerns about South Sudanese 'gangs' in Victoria and the community's difficulty in 'settling and adjusting to the Australian way of life' (quoted in Farouque et al., 2007; see also Due, 2008). The Minister's comments have been described as 'an appalling example of victim blaming', which 'established a benchmark for the vilification of African migrants' (Maher et al., 2018, p. 57).[11] Around this time, language used by the media to describe groups of African Australian young men – as 'mobs', 'packs', 'gangs' and 'thugs' (Windle, 2008) – reinforced the idea of them as a problem population. Racialised narratives about African criminality and 'gangs' were therefore already familiar to journalists, politicians and members of the Victorian electorate prior to the 2016 Moomba 'riot' (Majavu, 2018).

Moomba 2016 provided an opportunity for state politicians and local media outlets to amplify these racialised narratives and became a focal point for sections of the community to express their opposition to immigration from Africa more generally. Despite the widespread framing of 'African youth' as a problem, this issue was not influential in the state elections that took place in Victoria before the Moomba disturbances, in 2010 and 2014. But by 2018, the spectre of 'African crime' had become politicised. The main opposition party in the state election ran a concerted law and order campaign that capitalised on the fear of 'African crime', notably the emotion-filled crime of 'home invasion'. Rather than going 'behind the criminal acts to the conditions that are producing black crime as one of their effects', as advocated by Hall et al. (1978, p. 389), the media, the federal government and the Victorian state opposition aligned crime with blackness and a humanitarian migration crisis, as if these were the underlying causes.

Certainly, there is evidence that young men of Sudanese/South Sudanese background are over-represented in criminal justice institutions and crime statistics in Victoria (ABC Fact Check, 2018; Armytage & Ogloff, 2017); however, the over-representation of people from ethnic minorities in criminal justice institutions is a frequently observed reality in countries around the world. Framing a particular ethnic community as a problem group because its members account for a small, albeit disproportionate minority of offenders fails to acknowledge the systemic features and institutional practices that contribute to these statistics.[12] It is not our intention to try and explain this over-representation or to dissect the analyses of others who have attempted to do so. If this question interests our readers, then we would simply stress the need to look beyond reductionist explanations or simplistic hypotheses and consider how labelling processes and their effects may interact with, reproduce and amplify various 'risk factors' that have been linked to primary offending in marginalised communities. As argued elsewhere, the nature of these

---

[11]This incident has striking parallels with the furore that erupted in 1993 when a black British youth, Stephen Lawrence, was murdered in the streets of London by white nationalists. The initial handling of the incident, in which Stephen and his friend – a witness who survived the attack – were treated by police as suspects rather than victims, sparked the most significant enquiry into systemic racism in the London Metropolitan Police in recent history (McPherson, 1999).

[12]The Crime Statistics Agency in Victoria noted for the year ending September 2017 Sudanese-born offenders account for only 1% of the unique offender population (Crime Statistics Agency, 2018).

interactions is complex, as are the consequences of social exclusion, discrimination and labelling, which can affect not only young people but also entire communities for generations (Maher et al., 2020).

Our intention is rather to provide a multifaceted case study of one situated, contemporary law and order crisis, supported throughout by original empirical data. Individually and collectively, the authors have conducted research in Melbourne in the period following the disturbances at Moomba, covering the core topics of media representation, political communication, policing, racial hatred and the impacts of these processes on affected communities. This foundation of original empirical data, both qualitative and quantitative, has enabled a broad and integrated account of the genesis and implications of the law and order crisis about African youth crime in Victoria. While deeply rooted in local conditions, the book will resonate with similar instances of the criminalisation and othering of racialised communities and the rise of anti-immigration politics in many parts of the world.

About this Book

In this book we examine events both prior to and after the Moomba 'riot', charting the political debate around 'African crime' and 'African gangs' and presenting an integrated analysis of the social and political processes that combined to construct a 'crisis' at this particular time and place. We trace the contours of a highly racialised and politicised public discourse that portrayed young people of African heritage[13] as dangerous 'crimmigrants' and has had a profound impact on African Australian communities, policing practice and community dynamics. Many questions arise as a result of these events, not just about why this racialised campaign occurred and why this specific community was targeted but also about why it occurred in a city that is particularly proud of its diversity, multicultural image and heritage.[14] In addressing these questions, we hope to advance new understandings of the contradictions inherent in the search for collective security in a political and social climate that promotes social division, including along racial lines.

This book has its origins in a roundtable discussion that was part of the Australian and New Zealand Society of Criminology annual conference held at Melbourne University in December 2018. In the spirit of *Policing the Crisis*, the writing process has been a truly collaborative effort. Each of the authors had

---

[13]In this book we use a variety of terms including African Australian, South Sudanese/ Sudanese Australian, or simply African, South Sudanese or Sudanese to refer to these communities, depending on the context (see also footnote 2). The term 'Australian' does not equate to legal citizenship of Australia in these naming conventions, but is used primarily to indicate inclusion within Australian society.

[14]Demonisation of African Australians has occurred elsewhere (see, for example, the analysis by Palmer et al. (2020) of the criminalisation of Sudanese Australians in the state of Queensland). However, the process in Melbourne stands out as being particularly systematic and heightened by the high-profile 'riots' that are the cornerstone of our analysis.

independently conducted empirical research directed towards an aspect of the law and order crisis around 'African crime', including sustained collaborations with members of the affected communities. Although the conference was an academic event, and therefore not open to the wider community, several South Sudanese Australians who had participated in aspects of the research were invited to share their experiences and interpretations of the events directly.

After the discussion we formed the view that combining insights from our individual studies into one consolidated analysis could help to shed light on these extraordinary events. At the same time, we make no claim to speak on behalf of affected groups, who are not represented in the authorship.[15] Indeed, our focus throughout is on the contribution of institutions and key political actors and commentators to the construction of the 'crisis', not on the communities that were targeted by the 'African gangs' discourse. Where we do refer to the often devastating impacts of these events on African Australian communities, we rely on accounts provided to us in community-based research that was facilitated by grassroots organisations and community members. While the resulting book reflects the research and interpretations of a group of white academics, we hope that the analysis will contribute to scholarship on racialised othering, crimmi-gration, law and order politics, perceptions of risk and dangerousness and the uneven production of security within deeply stratified societies that are characterised by intense contestation over membership and belonging.

In Chapter 2, we consider the role of key political actors in generating a racialised media discourse in an attempt to construct a law and order election. Chapter 3 charts the ascendance of the 'African gangs' theme in media reporting following the Moomba events and examines how the tone and content of news media reporting contributed to the production of a sense of crisis. In Chapter 4, we consider how local police both responded to and reproduced the perception of African Australians as 'crimmigrant others' in one highly multicultural area of Melbourne. Chapter 5 examines the detrimental effect of these sustained exclusionary processes on community attitudes towards African Australians and the lasting impact on the sense of security and belonging experienced by South Sudanese Australians in particular.

With the exception of Chapter 2, which draws on documentary sources to account for the political construction of this law and order crisis, each chapter is built on a foundation of primary research data. In Chapter 3, we use Factiva to source relevant news reports from 2007 to the end of 2020. Here, we use a count of the frequency of articles to illustrate the trajectory of reports concerning the Sudanese/South Sudanese community over the time period of interest. A content analysis was then conducted on the 100 most relevant articles identified by Factiva. The material on community experiences of policing presented in Chapter 4 was

---

[15]Despite the presence of no less a figure than Jamaican-born Stuart Hall in the writing line-up, even *Policing the Crisis* attracted criticism some decades later for its failure to explicitly consider the positionality of its authors (Connell, 2015). However, the same critic considered the work to be an 'exemplar of engaged research' by virtue of the close involvement of the authors with affected communities (p. 279).

obtained through focus groups and interviews with youth workers and South Sudanese Australians in south-east Melbourne.[16] The data informing Chapter 5 originate from focus groups and interviews with Melbourne-based South Sudanese young people and mothers that were conducted for a study with the Melbourne-based Centre for Multicultural Youth (see Benier et al., 2018).

Collectively, the chapters address the following research questions:

- How did South Sudanese Australians in Melbourne come to be identified as a unique threat to community safety, particularly following the 2016 Moomba Festival?
- What was the role played by the media, state and federal politics, police and community perceptions of race in this process?
- What were the impacts on affected communities of the 'law and order crisis' concerning 'African crime' in terms of their own feelings of physical and emotional security?

While we do not lay claim to the level of grand theorising presented in *Policing the Crisis*, we hope this book illuminates some of the underlying processes at play, in ways that will have both local application and global relevance. Under the present conditions of advanced neoliberalism and rapid globalisation, many societies around the world are experiencing contestation over membership that is deepening social divisions on the basis of race, ethnicity, citizenship and other markers of difference. The failure to find socially inclusive solutions might be thought of as a 'crisis of multiculturalism', paralleling the 'crisis of capitalism' that underpinned the analysis made by Hall et al. at a time when these economic and social trends were beginning to emerge.

We acknowledge that matters of political economy are under-developed in our analysis, since none of the research conducted by the authors directly incorporated this perspective. Similarly, readers may find that in focussing on racial attributions and immigration status, other important aspects of identity such as gender and socioeconomic status have received less attention than may be warranted. Nevertheless, by bringing together a comprehensive body of empirical evidence addressing the construction of a 'law and order crisis' about so-called African crime and updating the analytical tools used to consider how and why particular African Australian communities were targeted and with what implications, we hope not only to shed light on these specific events but also to develop new theories about processes of racialised othering and the construction of 'crimmigrants' that is applicable to increasingly multicultural, technologically enabled and globally interconnected societies.

---

[16]Australian Research Council Future Fellowship 'Globalisation and the policing of internal borders' (FT140101044).

Chapter 2

From 'Apex' to '#AfricanGangs'

In this chapter we trace the roots of the 'law and order crisis' that occurred in the lead-up to the 2018 Victorian state election to the so-called Moomba riot of 2016.[1] This event and its aftermath appeared to merge and bring to a head two sources of social anxiety: a sense of fear about rising youth violence and a youth justice system in crisis in the months prior; and a generalised suspicion of Melbourne's Sudanese/South Sudanese communities and their alleged 'failure to integrate', which had been smouldering over the preceding decade.[2] These currents converged into a stream of antipathy and demonisation that was fuelled by media distortion and exaggeration, the politicisation of crime control and its connection to immigration debates and the resultant sense of public unease.

The events of Moomba 2016 thus precipitated a sense of imminent *and* immanent threat of disorder, both associated with a generalised other: the 'violent young offender' striking fear into suburban hearts and the African Australian who did not quite fit in with white and multicultural Australia's sense of itself. The two sides of this mythic 'other' converged in the public mind and took embodied form in 'South Sudanese youth', of which the 'Apex gang' represented the epitome. Here we invoke Hallsworth and Young's (2008, pp. 184–185, emphasis in original) important reminder that '[t]he term gang signifies not this or that group out there but a *Monstrous Other*, an organized counter force confronting the good society...'.

Throughout this chapter, we reflect on the normative fulcrum of 'the good society' – how it supports narratives about *who we are* as a community and *who we want to be* as a country – to locate the anatomy of this rising panic against the discursive backdrop of a law and order crisis and the rise of penal populism. This context provides insight into divisive discourses about *who we want to live here*, a trope that John Howard famously legitimised in his 2001 election speech and which

---

[1]Since the previous state election, in 2014, the Labor Party was in government in Victoria and the conservative Liberal–Nationals Coalition was in opposition. The Greens held two seats in the lower house of parliament.

[2]Kevin Andrews was reported as saying: 'some groups don't seem to be settling and adjusting into the Australian way of life' (Farouque et al., 2007).

Place, Race and Politics, 23–40
Copyright © 2021 Leanne Weber, Jarrett Blaustein, Kathryn Benier, Rebecca Wickes and Diana Johns
Published under exclusive licence by Emerald Publishing Limited
doi:10.1108/978-1-80043-045-720211002

is historically rooted in the racist White Australia policy (Jayasuriya et al., 2003).[3] Thus, in the tradition of Hall et al. (1978, p. viii), we seek to examine how *race, crime* and *youth* – condensed into the image of 'Sudanese thugs' and 'African gangs' – came to serve as the 'ideological conductor'. As a starting point, we canvass the literature on penal populism, which provides several useful concepts for theorising and contextualising the political construction of the 'African gangs' crisis.

Penal Populism and 'Law and Order Auctions'

Embedded in notions of 'the good society', law and order has been a prominent political issue in Anglophone democracies since (at least) the 1960s. Each election is unique, of course, but the overarching political dynamics of a law and order election might be summarised thus: conservative candidates attempt to elevate law and order issues to the top of the political agenda and progressive opponents then respond by adopting their own outwardly punitive policy platforms, lest they appear weak and ineffective on crime. Politicians' perception that the 'failure to talk tough on crime is akin to political suicide' very often gives rise to what Newburn and Jones (2005, p. 74) describe as a 'populist punitive bipartisan consensus', which prompts consideration of the rise of penal populism during the later half of the twentieth century.

Penal populism refers to the phenomenon of 'politicians tapping into, and using for their own purposes, what they believe to be the public's generally punitive stance' (Bottoms, 1995, p. 40). Penal theorists have sought to explain this trend in terms of broader social, economic, political and cultural shifts associated with life in late modernity (Garland, 2001; Taylor, 1999), the rise of neoliberal penality (O'Malley, 1994; Pratt, 1998; Wacquant, 2001a, 2009), the institutional structure of democratic systems (Barker, 2009; Lacey, 2008; Miller, 2008) and, more locally, the influence of lobbyists (Page, 2011) and victims' rights movements (Dubber, 2002). Some analyses have shown how the politics of crime and criminal justice have become increasingly noxious and 'uncivil' (Hogg & Brown, 1998) and how the politicisation of crime control has been shaped by the cultural politics of exclusion (Taylor, 1999; Young, 1999) and the deeply racialised criminalisation of poverty, minorities and immigrants (Wacquant, 1999, 2001a, 2001b, 2002).

Although the causes of penal populism are complex and contextually bound, its punitive consequences are often similar. Criminal justice and penal policies in many jurisdictions have become increasingly responsive to politicians' perceptions of public opinion (real, imagined or invented) rather than pragmatic or humane

---

[3]John Howard, 28 October 2001: 'we will decide who comes to this country and the circumstances in which they come' (https://electionspeeches.moadoph.gov.au/speeches/2001-john-howard) in response to the 'Tampa affair' of August 2001 (see https://theconversation.com/australian-politics-explainer-the-mv-tampa-and-the-transformation-of-asylum-seeker-policy-74078).

crime-reducing strategies. These policies have contributed to significant increases in the use of imprisonment across Anglophone democracies since the 1970s and manifest most starkly in America's mass incarceration. Given that the heaviest impacts fall on racialised minorities, some scholars argue that punitive policies and practices arising from penal populism are not novel historical developments but, rather, contemporary manifestations of deep-rooted historical patterns of racialised social control (Alexander, 2010; Cunneen, 2001; Wacquant, 2002). Accordingly, critical scholars have long argued that marginalised populations provide opportunistic political elites with convenient others or 'folk devils' to blame for insecurities resulting from economic and social inequality in post-industrial societies (Bauman, 2000; Hall et al., 1978).

A Political 'Blueprint'

In the United States, the recent history of penal populism and 'law and order' as a political issue might be traced to 1964, when Republican presidential candidate Barry Goldwater campaigned on a platform of law and order to capitalise on rising anxiety about crime and the civil rights movement among white voters (Newburn & Jones, 2005). While Goldwater was ultimately unsuccessful in his presidential bid, the platform subsequently became a staple of the Republican electoral playbook because it was clear that the Democrats' agenda, which focussed on addressing the underlying causes of crime and civil disorder through social welfare programmes, was becoming increasingly unpopular with voters (Chambliss, 1999).

Twenty-four years later, the successful 1988 presidential campaign of George Bush Sr represented one of the most effective uses of law and order politics in American politics. One of Bush's key messages was that his Democratic opponent, Michael Dukakis, was 'soft' and 'weak' on several issues including crime (Newburn & Jones, 2005). The centrepiece of the 1988 campaign was a series of television advertisements that deployed sensationalist, heavily racialised and in some cases factually inaccurate messaging and imagery to emphasise the contrast between these two candidates. Specifically, the notorious 'Willie Horton' campaign ad used 'sinister images of the black rapist of a white woman as emblematic of the contemporary "crime problem"' (Wacquant, 2002, p. 43). Bush won the presidency in a landslide victory that November.

Dukakis's loss ushered in a new era of law and order politics in the United States as Democratic candidates quickly realised that 'liberal' policies had become politically untenable. Bill Clinton's pre-emptive 'tough on crime' position was a factor in his 1992 electoral success and, throughout his two-term presidency, Clinton sustained this image with a number of crime control policies including a federal 'three-strikes law' that formed part of the *1994 Crime Bill* (Marion, 1997; Newburn & Jones, 2005). Clinton thus established a blueprint for centrist-Democratic politicians seeking to neutralise the political consequences of law and order politics in the United States. These global currents are important because they seep into and impregnate political debates in other jurisdictions.

In 1990s Britain, for instance, Tony Blair actively modelled elements of the 'New Labour' platform on Clinton's success: Blair's policy mantra − 'tough on crime and tough on the causes of crime' − emphasised his law and order credentials while appealing to Labour's traditional progressive support base (Newburn & Jones, 2005; Newburn, 2007; Tonry, 2004). This platform, which characterised Blair's 1997 electoral campaign and New Labour policies throughout the 2000s, also shaped political developments in Australia. Weatherburn (2004) notes that, in a series of 'law and order auctions' − political parties trying to outbid each other in terms of crime control policy following several high-profile criminal incidents that attracted significant media attention − progressive politicians, in seeking to balance 'both the popular demand for harsh treatment of serious or persistent offenders and the rising public thirst for a more enlightened approach' (p. 44), emulated Blair's approach.

Another aspect of New Labour logic that took hold in Australia was the discourse of 'evidence-based policy' that, on the one hand, embedded evaluation in government service delivery as a means of ensuring efficiency and accountability and, on the other, provided political decision-making and managerialism with a veneer of 'scientific' objectivity and legitimacy (Travers, 2005). With this new-found source of confidence, in the 'law and order auctions' that ensued across Australia during the late 1990s and early 2000s, centre-left governments of the Australian Labor Party (henceforth, Labor) frequently espoused outwardly punitive policies and committed vast sums of money to policing and/or prisons in order to neutralise criticism from conservative opponents (Hogg & Brown, 1998; Weatherburn, 2004).

Governing through Race, Crime and Youth

One explanation for progressive governments' shift towards penal populism is Simon's (2007) 'governing through crime' thesis, though, as Cunneen (2011, p. 11) suggests, in settler-colonial countries like Australia, the notion of 'colonising and racialising through crime' may be as germane. Indeed, Wacquant (2002, p. 44) argues, it is *not* 'crime, but the need to shore up an eroding [deeply racialised] caste cleavage' that has driven penal expansionism. Perhaps more usefully, as Simon (2002) claims, we can think of crime as a 'governmental metaphor' (p. 1039), narrated for specific purposes. The task is then to ascertain what those purposes might be and whose interests they serve. Simon certainly shows how crime has been used to generate and structure responses to 'idealized and demonized legal subjects' (Fleury-Steiner et al., 2009, p. 6), but not specifically how race and racism is embedded and 'routinized' (p. 7) in everyday criminal justice assumptions, practices and processes.

With this aim, Fleury-Steiner et al. (2009, p. 8) show how 'a racist common sense of crime and criminals' is produced through the combined institutional logics of law enforcement, politicians and media organisations. While negating explicitly racist motives on the part of media operators, they reveal how media representations nevertheless structure and embed racism by encoding and reproducing conservative fears and middle-class anxieties about urban and social decay and disorder. From this perspective, media, criminal justice actors and politicians – 'tapping into, and using for their own purposes, what they believe to be the public's generally punitive stance' (Bottoms, 1995, p. 40) – distance themselves from overt racism by coding difference in terms of risk and danger and the 'defence of mythical "good" places and persons' (Fleury-Steiner et al., 2009, p. 6).

Consequently, as Lianos and Douglas (2000) observe, '[t]he debate field of "law and order", increasingly exploited politically, is more about *order* than law and even more about *insecurity*' (p. 274, our emphasis), frequently coded as 'safety'. This is where *race, crime* and *youth* come into play, as generalised threats to order and safety and cultural scripts for constructing 'folk devils' who represent a danger to the 'good society'. As Lianos and Douglas (2000, pp. 272–273) explain:

> Race, age, gender and poverty are being recast in the mould of dangerousness, which now becomes the emerging category for legitimizing social exclusion. … visible qualities which can be associated with the lower classes – such as race or subcultural attitudes – become automatic indicators of dangerousness.

From this perspective, racialised young men are perceived as 'threats' based on their appearance and behaviour. These 'visible qualities' then become legitimate targets of strategies to assert control and establish order *and* measures of those strategies' 'success'. 'In the days, weeks and months following Moomba 2016', for instance, as *The Age* reported, 'a taskforce was created, arrests were made, charges laid and some of the young men were thrown into detention centres. A special court was set up to deal with the large number of offenders involved' (Woods, 2017a). This swift youth justice response manifested Premier Andrews's vow that those responsible for the Moomba violence would 'feel the full force of the law' (in Willingham & Preiss, 2016). This demonstrates the common sense logic of crime and justice while both the threat and the response were clearly racialised in terms of the explicit association with African background young men. The visible difference of *some* African Australian young people involved in *some* violence drove a wider perception of *all* black African youth as 'risky' and dangerous.

For lawmakers and law-enforcers, the 'projection of menace … becomes a contemporary way of building institutional legitimacy' (Lianos & Douglas, 2000, p. 269). 'Danger-based legitimacy' (2000, p. 269) is garnered through strategies of control, such as punitive justice measures. But this dangerisation process is not seen as racial discrimination because it is coded as community safety, public order and individual security. Race is 'laundered' through risk (Goddard & Myers, 2017). And risk establishes safety as a mode of political governance (Lianos, 2013) that to middle-class progressives is palatable, tolerable and indeed entirely reasonable.

Otherness as a Category of Menace

Danger or menace is tied to behaviours that mark those who *do not belong*. Belonging here evokes boundaries, 'us' and 'them' judgements (Yuval-Davis,

2006). For Lianos (2013) this *otherness* is grounded in insecurity. The conditions of late modernity generate ontological and material insecurity (Young, 1999) in ways that bring us together yet pit us against each other, whereby otherness becomes 'a marker of fear and lack of social confidence' that generates 'a constant quest for security and safety' (Lianos, 2013, p. 1). Others are objects of fear and distrust, while '*those like oneself belong* by definition to *an automatically legitimized category*' (p. 1, our emphasis).

Here it is important to recall the suspicion and apprehension with which newly arrived African communities were received in Victoria during the 1990s and 2000s (Windle, 2008), and which Kevin Andrews expressed at the federal level with his 2007 comments about South Sudanese people's 'failure to integrate'. If belonging is the criterion for security and safety, and a social group is seen to *not belong* on the grounds of their appearance or perceived difference, then their otherness becomes 'a category of menace' (Lianos & Douglas, 2000).

In this use of categorisation to invoke threat, Young's (1999) two motifs of exclusion are apparent — 'the actuarial and the demonising: one calculative and cool and the other essentializing and judgemental' (p. 387). Together, these two forces can explain the targeting of racialised 'others' in ways that seemingly negate their race yet, at the same time, identify and categorise the risk associated with their otherness in terms of perceived *difference* and *difficulty* (that is, crime, disorder, incivility) (Young, 1999, p. 389). This offers a way of understanding punitiveness — in discourse and practice, narrative and policy — as grounded in legitimising rationales of safety and risk management, across the political spectrum.

As criminologists, in explaining the 'law and order crisis' that took hold in Victoria leading up to the 2018 election, we might easily fall into reproducing worn-out, shallow accounts of 'moral panic', 'penal populism' or even what O'Malley (2000) calls 'criminologies of catastrophe'. Instead, to go beyond broad-brush description and explain *in local detail* a specific time and place, we examine how the myths and images of 'Apex' and 'African gangs' essentialised and sublimated racialised youth crime as the 'ideological conductor' of a law and order 'crisis' in Victoria (Hall et al., 1978). With the remainder of this chapter, we analyse media reports and political statements surrounding the events of Moomba 2016 to trace how these currents became charged through media exaggeration, distortion and politicisation and condensed into images of 'Apex' and 'African gangs'.

'Victoria under Labor'

The disorder at Moomba was widely reported in the Victorian media and, on the following morning, Opposition Leader Matthew Guy (Leader of the Liberal Party, henceforth Liberals, in the Victorian Liberal–National Coalition) tweeted:

> When you are fine with 'passive' Policing, non pursuit policies and closing stations it ends up with riots at Moomba. Victoria under Labor.
>
> (@MatthewGuyMP, 13 March 2016a)

The tweet highlights that the Liberals were quick to blame the inability of Victoria Police to prevent this disorder on the policies of the Andrews government. 'Passive' policing was framed as a consequence of Labor's 'soft on crime' policies and failure to adequately resource police. Along these lines, the Opposition Police Spokesman Edward O'Donohue, quoted in a *Herald Sun* article, would similarly assert that 'Victoria Police are critically under-resourced and stretched, and they can only deploy the resources at their disposal' (Galloway et al., 2016). The same *Herald Sun* article went on to suggest that what happened at Moomba was part of a wider crime problem, linking the disorder to the so-called Apex gang's alleged involvement in a series of car thefts and home invasions that had occurred throughout the city's south-eastern suburbs since June of 2015 (Galloway et al., 2016). This narrative effectively projected the menace of this 'gang' onto Melbourne's recent spike in violent offending and dangerised and solidified the status of Apex as the folk devil of the Moomba 'riot', which then remained a fixture of the tabloid media in Victoria for more than a year.[4]

In response to these claims, Labor Premier Daniel Andrews staged a press conference on 14 March 2016 where he predictably adopted a hard-line stance towards the perpetrators, emphasising the legitimacy of law enforcement in regaining order and control:

> What occurred on Saturday night is completely unacceptable. I will make sure that Victoria Police has whatever they need to smash these gangs and make sure we don't have a repeat. ... It does not matter who you are, your circumstances, your background, if you break the law you feel the full force of the law.
>
> (Victorian Premier Daniel Andrews, quoted in Willingham & Preiss, 2016)

Further emphasis on the menace of 'the perpetrators' and their 'unacceptable' behaviour was added to this message by the caption that the Premier used to tweet this article, 'choice' seeming to underscore the threat of implied malevolence:

> For the perpetrators, Saturday night was a choice – and it's one they will regret.
>
> (@DanielAndrewsMP, 2016)

This memorably succinct political sound bite conspicuously echoes the tone of former Conservative Prime Minister David Cameron in the wake of the 2011 England riots:

---

[4]According to the Crime Statistics Agency, while offending by people aged 10–24 years had dropped overall, 2015–2016 saw a slight increase in young people engaging in high-frequency reoffending (Millsteed & Sutherland, 2016). At the same time, three of the authors have previously noted that neither 'Apex' nor South Sudanese Australians had been in the media spotlight during the two-year period preceding the Moomba 'riot' (Benier et al., 2018).

This is criminality, pure and simple, and it has to be confronted and defeated.

(Quoted in Newburn et al., 2018)

Far from coincidental similarity, we argue that both statements were constructed to locate responsibility squarely with the perpetrators and to emphasise the government's swift and decisive response. For Cameron, this framing served to deflect attention away from the socioeconomic grievances of the rioters and the impact of austerity policies on both disadvantaged communities and policing. For Andrews, it was, in the first instance, a rebuttal to the suggestion that Labor was soft on crime. Nevertheless, in invoking a seemingly calm and measured response, Labor's rebuttal served to validate the danger, together with the necessity for re-establishing order, control and safety.

Andrews's immediate response took the form of Taskforce Ares, which was established to identify and arrest the perpetrators using CCTV footage. This can be interpreted as the state government ostensibly performing its capability to control and arrest. This occurred two days after the Moomba 'riot' and Premier Andrews was immediately criticised on social media by the Shadow Minister for Police for taking too long to act and putting additional strain on Victoria Police personnel who established the taskforce (O'Donohue, 2016). Over the next six weeks, 34 people, 33 of whom were under the age of 18, were charged with various offences including 'affray, riotous behaviour, offensive behaviour, assault, robbery and theft' (Cowie, 2016). Throughout the investigation, however, senior police officers repeatedly attempted to debunk the idea that this was an 'African' problem, with one Assistant Commissioner going so far as to describe Apex as 'the United Nations' of offending and a 'melting pot' (see SBS, 2016).

These attempts to deracialise the problem were echoed in the police use of 'the research' to support their operational decisions, as Assistant Commissioner Leane's comments suggest:

We've had young people who may never have been in contact with police before accelerating their criminal behaviours in a way we haven't seen, and that's a significant challenge for us. … If they become serial offenders as a child more than likely, *the research says*, they move into continued lifelong criminal offending. That is a real risk for our community.

(Hosking, 2016, emphasis added)

This reference to 'the research' to explain and justify their responses implies that police work is grounded in scientific evidence and can also be interpreted as police efforts to legitimise their expertise in the face of 'a significant challenge' and 'a real risk' (that is, danger). While eager to capitalise on the window of opportunity created by Moomba, even the Opposition was initially careful to avoid explicitly racialising this issue. Accordingly, their messaging centred on three themes: the Andrews government's *failure* to adequately resource police, *unwillingness* to acknowledge that Victoria had a crime problem and *inability* to craft an effective law and order response. This narrative of out-of-control disorder was encapsulated in a tweet by Opposition Leader Matthew Guy on 16 March 2016:

Life under Labor: Crime skyrocketing, Police numbers cut and stations closing. Gang violence, random shootings. #hiremorepolice.

(Guy, 2016b)

'...Profound Investments in a Safer and Stronger Victoria'

Despite the visibility of Taskforce Ares and its purported success, crime remained at the top of the political agenda in Victoria. We attribute the persistence of this issue to the fact that subsequent criminal incidents, reportedly perpetrated by 'Apex' members, continued to attract media coverage and commentary from the Liberal–National Opposition. The Andrews government needed to be seen to act and this created a policy window that in turn prompted the local tabloid, the *Herald Sun*, to sponsor a Youth Summit in partnership with the Chief Commissioner of Victoria Police Graham Ashton in July 2016. The event was attended by more than 200 people – representatives from government, not-for-profit organisations and prominent members of the community – who came together to discuss the issue and put forth recommendations to the government. Ashton reportedly emphasised finding ways 'that will keep our community safe', while the *Herald Sun* reportedly highlighted the 'proliferation of youth crime' as 'one of the biggest social and legal challenges facing Victoria' and asserted their aim 'to bring an unprecedented community focus on the issues driving the [youth crime] problem' (Hosking, 2016). Though the official narrative was thus becoming deracialised, the 'youth crime' narrative could still have the effect of dangerising those seen as responsible for 'the problem': in the public mind, at least, the mythologised 'Apex'.

In his welcoming address, Ashton acknowledged the existence of a wider youth crime problem by stating that real changes were occurring with respect to the nature, severity and frequency of youth offending in Victoria. He directly acknowledged the 'mob behaviour' at Moomba as a source of concern for the Victorian public but noted that the roots of the problem went deeper: social exclusion, disengagement from school, association with problematic peers, financial hardship, being 'locked out' of social and economic opportunities and a lack of family support. The race, ethnicity and migration status of the perpetrators did not feature in Ashton's comments and, as evident from a retrospective search of the event's Twitter hashtag (#vicpolsummit) and one of the authors' personal reflections of the event, were not a dominant focus of the discussions. Rather, the takeaway message was that youth crime was a complex problem that necessitated a holistic response, albeit an immediate one (ABC News, 2016).

The tempered proceedings of the Youth Summit nevertheless had a significant policy impact as recommendations from this event directly informed a raft of punitive youth justice reforms announced by the Andrews government on 5 December 2016. The *Children and Justice Legislation (Youth Justice Reform) Bill 2017* included proposals to increase from three years to four years the maximum period of detention for young offenders, create a Youth Control Order ('a more intensive and targeted supervision sentence for young offenders'), establish an Intensive Monitoring and Control Bail Supervision Scheme, introduce new reporting and information-sharing requirements relating to the behaviour of young people in detention and extend the Youth Justice Bail Supervision scheme (Andrews, 2016).

Two days later, the Andrews government also announced Victoria's first-ever comprehensive Community Safety Plan at a press conference with Victoria Police. Key initiatives and reforms included a commitment of $2 billion in funding to modernise the police and stimulate recruitment of frontline officers, a $32-million youth reform package including $10 million in grants for community-based programmes focussing on prevention and diversion, the creation of a 24-hour police assistance line for non-emergency calls and authorisation for police officers to collect DNA from suspects without a warrant (see Victoria Police, 2016). Labor thus addressed both welfarist and punitive youth justice demands in a sweeping set of reforms that set a firm 'no-nonsense' tone. Announcing this reform package at a press conference, Andrews responded to the Opposition's criticisms by stating:

> We have always said, and we've meant it every time, that we would give the chief commissioner the resources he needs, the powers he needs, to fight crime and keep our community safe. ... All of these are not costs, they're profound investments in a safer and stronger Victoria.
>
> (Victoria Police, 2016)

Labor's message was that they are responsive to public concerns about crime and willing to make a significant financial investment in the future of Victoria Police and the youth justice system. The message emphasised order, safety and strength and − in invoking the state's power to punish − slips in a typically criminalising 'us and them' trope that infers a boundary between lawbreakers and the law-abiding. By comparison, Newburn et al.'s (2018) analysis of the aftermath of the 2011 England riots determined that the Coalition government's commitment to its platform of austerity limited its policy options in the wake of this event. Perhaps the ability and willingness of the Andrews government to engage in a 'law and order auction' (Weatherburn, 2004) − to outbid the Opposition in heavily criminalising responses while also pledging more progressive approaches − explains in part why this political focussing event (Kingdon, 1984) contributed to concrete policy changes.

'Making Victoria Safe Again'

As the Liberal–National Opposition actively worked to keep law and order at the top of the political agenda in Victoria throughout 2017, the longevity of this issue is perhaps best explained by the local media's ongoing sensationalist and heavily racialised coverage of criminal incidents involving young people 'of African appearance' (see Chapter 3; also Koumouris & Blaustein, 2021). The incidents that were reported by journalists at the *Herald Sun* and linked to Apex included further 'riots' at the state's youth justice facilities in January and February (see, for example, Travers, 2017), a 'possible large-scale riot' involving 'gangs of youth' that was 'thwarted' by police at the city's White Night celebrations in February (Travers & Hosking, 2017) and a wave of carjackings and home invasions in the city's suburbs during 2015–2016 (Buttler & Galloway, 2016). It was around this time that the *Herald Sun* published a series of exposés about the so-called Apex gang. One such article described how another 16-year-old boy, reportedly a member of Apex, 'recently won an appeal to have his sentence cut for almost 80 charges' and 'also had time slashed because of a clerical error in sentencing' (Thompson, 2017). The message was that Victoria's youth justice system was too lenient and thus unable to achieve deterrence, reform or even incapacitation of these 'gangs'.

The Liberals' ability to keep law and order at the top of the political agenda was bolstered by the media's coverage of unrelated incidents that contributed to Victorians' growing sense of fear and insecurity. For example, the issue of bail reform gained further political momentum in the aftermath of an unrelated attack that occurred on 20 January 2017, when a 26-year-old man who had been granted bail against the advice of the police deliberately drove his car into a crowd of pedestrians in Melbourne's CBD, killing 6 and injuring 27 people. In a media release issued just three days after this attack, Matthew Guy linked this attack to 'Apex' in calling for 'the reinstatement of the offence of breaching bail by juveniles which was a change that weakened our bail system in 2016' (Guy, 2017a). The rationale he later provided was that 'the Andrews government repealed the law that made it an offence for juvenile offenders, including members of the Apex gang, to breach their bail' (Guy, 2017b). This statement was intended to signal that the justice reform initiatives that had been announced by the Andrews government following the Youth Summit were weak and insufficient.

Thus, in a further attempt to signal his government's law and order credentials and assert his government's ability to take things in hand, Andrews announced a major restructuring of youth justice in February 2017 (Andrews, 2017). While, historically, the state's youth justice system had been managed by the Department of Health and Human Services (DHHS), it would henceforth be run by the Department of Justice and Regulation, which was responsible for adult corrections. At the same time, Andrews announced plans to build a new $288-million high-security youth justice centre with 224 beds. Outlining the rationale for these changes, Andrews stated: 'These reforms are what's needed to help keep the community safe and ensure the security of our youth justice facilities' (Andrews, 2017). In so clearly emphasising safety and security, Andrews was relying on the public's shared perception of danger to legitimise such massive expenditure (albeit in the face of increasing evidence against imprisonment as an effective response to youth offending). Andrews highlighted the economic benefits of the proposed youth justice centre, suggesting the project would generate between 2000 and 3000 jobs (Andrews, 2017), thereby linking Labor's law and order policies with its ongoing commitment to Victoria's economic growth through infrastructure development, seeking once again to build broad political appeal.

Once again, Guy persisted with his deficit-based 'safety' and 'order' message: 'Victoria is now a significantly less safe place to live, work and raise a family than it was two years ago' (Guy, 2017b). Addressing his traditional support base in the *Herald Sun*, he went on to promise:

> If I am Premier, I won't be a spectator while crime and violence engulfs our community. The Liberal Nationals have developed practical policies to *make Victoria safe again* … If I am Premier, *making Victoria safe again* will be my first, second and third priority.
>
> (Guy, 2017b, emphasis added)

This 'projection of menace at a large scale' – of crime and violence engulfing our community – yet coded in avuncular terms of 'practical policies' and 'making Victoria safe', can be seen as a clear bid for institutional legitimacy (Lianos & Douglas, 2000), riding on United States President Donald Trump's 'Make America Great Again' slogan. Guy's repeated reference to this phrase should be read as an attempt to link this law and order 'crisis' (also quoting Guy, 2017b) to emergent populist critiques of progressive values and policies. Characterising the Liberal–Nationals' proposals as 'practical' implied that the Andrews government policies announced in December remained idealistic and grounded in a progressive ideology that meant they were destined to fail. This message, together with repeated references to the Apex gang – which Victoria Police no longer believed to exist at this time (see Leane quoted in Travers & Hosking, 2017) – enabled the Coalition to capitalise on the *Herald Sun*'s ongoing racialised coverage of youth crime, without explicitly referring to the ethnicity of the alleged perpetrators. 'Laundering' race in this way, sanitising their exclusionary message for a conservative yet multicultural audience, was strategically important for the Coalition, who could not risk being branded racist or xenophobic in an electorate where 49.1% of Victorians had at least one parent born overseas (ABS, 2016). Simply, the Liberal–Nationals' law and order platform had to at least appear colour blind lest it alienate the Coalition's moderate support base.

Over the next few months, the Liberal–Nationals not only persisted in their criticism of the Andrews government's response to the law and order crisis but also actively sought to thwart Labor's attempts to get the *Children and Justice Legislation (Youth Justice Reform) Bill 2017* through Parliament. Ironically, this resistance was welcomed by many progressive supporters of the Andrews government, including criminologists who were concerned about the punitive and likely net-widening effect of proposed measures, including the introduction of Youth Control Orders and new powers for Protective Services Officers. In an open letter signed by 50 key stakeholders, it was noted that '[s]ome measures introduced by the bills are not evidence based' and threaten the future of Victoria's unique dual-track sentencing model, described as 'the foundation of our youth justice system' (Law Institute of Victoria, 2017). Despite these concerns and the Opposition's initial resistance to the legislation, the *Children and Justice Legislation (Youth Justice Reform) Bill 2017* was passed in September 2017.

'Lawlessness in Victoria'

Victoria's purported gang problem re-emerged in the media two months later following the publication of crime statistics in the *Herald Sun* which were presented in such a way as to suggest that there had been a significant increase in the number of 'Sudanese-born criminals' between the years 2014–2015 and 2016–2017 living in Victoria (see Smethurst & Buttler, 2017). Shortly after this article was published, the Parliamentary Joint Standing Committee on Migration published its report on migrant settlement outcomes, which included a section on 'Migrant Youth' (Joint Standing Committee on Migration, 2017, sec. 7) that claimed that Victoria had experienced 'an increase in gang activity involving youth' (par. 7.2) and that 'Sudanese-born offenders' were significantly over-represented in the crime statistics. The Chair of the Joint Standing Committee was later quoted in *The Australian*, a national conservative newspaper, as saying:

> A lot of migrants have no understanding of the law. I was told by South Sudanese people that … [*sic*] breaking into someone's house and stealing a car is not a big deal.
>
> (Wood quoted in Akerman, 2017)

The article then went on to cite figures obtained from Victoria's Crime Statistics Agency which showed that 'Sudanese and South Sudanese people were 6.135 times more likely to have been arrested last year than offenders born in Australia' (Akerman, 2017).

Statistics that featured in the Joint Standing Committee's report were subsequently corrected (Crime Statistics Agency, 2018) and a counter report by two federal Labor MPs claimed that it 'unfairly maligns Sudanese born youth in Victoria' (Vamvakinou & Neumann, 2018). Nevertheless, during the weeks that followed, a series of articles published in the *Herald Sun* reinvigorated the idea that there was an 'African crime problem' in Melbourne. The state-level Opposition responded in predictable fashion, with the Shadow Attorney-General John Pesutto asserting on television that 'there is clearly now an overrepresentation in gang related violence in Victoria by South Sudanese youths, that's a fact' (Pesutto on Sky News Australia, 2017). We believe this was one of the first explicit references to the ethnicity of the alleged problem group made by a state Liberal–Nationals politician.

The explicit racialisation of this problem quickly escalated as federal ministers from the Liberal–National Coalition government chimed in on the debate in order to sway the Victorian state election result and, more importantly, to reframe Victoria's so-called African gang problem as a consequence of a wider crisis of migration and multiculturalism in Australia. On 1 January, Australia's Prime Minister Malcolm Turnbull and Federal Minister Greg Hunt (from Victoria) addressed the issue at a press conference. Turnbull stated:

> We are very concerned at the growing gang violence and lawlessness in Victoria, in particular in Melbourne. This is a failure of the Andrews Government.
>
> (ABC News, 2018)

Turnbull's remarks were immediately followed by Hunt's explicit racialised framing of the problem:

> Gang crime in Victoria is clearly out of control. We know that African gang crime in some areas in particular, is clearly out of control. And the failure is not the police, but the Premier. The Victorian Government under Premier Andrews has dropped the ball on allowing the police to take a strong clear role.
>
> (ABC News, 2018)

Both Premier Andrews and Commissioner Ashton were on leave at the time.

In response to Hunt's statement, Labor and Victoria Police hastily organised a joint press conference featuring the Acting Commissioner and the Police Minister. Breaking with the official line, the Acting Commissioner openly acknowledged the 'overrepresentation by African youth in serious and violent offending as well as public disorder issues', while the Police Minister (in her response to a reporter's question) made the blunder of misnaming the Acting Premier (Victoria Police, 2018). Immediately, the *Herald Sun* reported the press conference as an admission by Victoria Police and Labor that there had been an 'African youth crime' problem in Melbourne all along (Minear et al., 2018). The same article reported that the Andrews government was becoming increasingly nervous about the fact that 'this African gang violence issue is still running', with an election only months away (quoting an 'anonymous MP' in Minear et al., 2018). In response to the Police Minister's blunder, Guy tweeted:

> The Police Minister admits – in the middle of a law and order and African gang crisis – that she has no idea who is in charge of the state as Andrews, Merlino and Allen are all MIA ['missing in action'].
>
> (Guy, 2018)

Less than a year away from the November election, race and migration were now the front and centre in the political debate about youth crime in Victoria. While this could be read as increasing desperation on the part of the conservative Opposition, since Labor was gaining ground on issues of order and safety, it still created a significant dilemma for the Andrews government. On the one hand, the government was facing significant pressure to amplify its punitive response and direct it towards this 'problem group'. On the other hand, conceding that there was an 'African gangs' problem in Victoria risked alienating its ethnically diverse support base and losing seats to the Greens Party, which was seen to be a potential electoral threat at the time.

#AfricanGangs

Labor's political reprieve came almost immediately, thanks to an opportunity created by a significant public backlash to the explicitly racialised 'African gangs' frame following widely publicised comments made by the Federal Minister for Home Affairs, Peter Dutton, during a Sydney radio interview on 3 January 2018:

> People don't see this in New South Wales and Queensland, but the reality is, you know, people are scared to go out to restaurants in the night-time because they're followed home by these gangs, home invasions, and cars are stolen. We just need to call it for what it is: African gang violence.... We need to weed out the people who've done the wrong thing, deport them where we can, but where they're Australian citizens, we need to deal with them according to the law.
>
> (Dutton on 2GB – see Kenny, 2018)

Over the next few days, Victorians, including Acting Premier Daniel Bowen, tweeted photos of their dinners with the hashtag #MelbourneBitesBack to ridicule Dutton's suggestion that 'people are scared to go out in the night-time'. Dutton had gone too far, and as racist stereotyping burgeoned on social media under the hashtag #AfricanGangs, even state Liberal candidates, including Guy, attempted to distance themselves from the explicitly racialised framing. To this end, Guy stated: 'It's not about *African* gangs, it's about gangs full-stop' (Guy quoted in Tomazin, 2018). Days later, an informal Twitter campaign reclaimed the #AfricanGangs hashtag, as members of Victoria's African Australian communities shared photos of their friends and families participating in everyday activities to showcase their accomplishments and counter the negative depiction of their communities (see Wahlquist, 2018a).

When Chief Commissioner Ashton returned to work on 10 January, he immediately organised a press conference with prominent members of the African Australian community. Ashton expressed concern about 'law-abiding' members of this community being subject to racial abuse due to recent political remarks and attributed this to the media's inflammatory coverage of this 'crisis'. Ashton also announced that he was forming a police–community taskforce to address this issue and, to the surprise of many, directly dismissed Dutton's comments as 'utter garbage' (Ashton quoted in Bucci, 2018). On the following day, Andrews returned to work and provided a further repudiation of Dutton's comments by suggesting that they 'were designed to get a rise out of people ... they were designed to be as controversial as possible' (Andrews quoted in Wahlquist, 2018b).

On 24 November, Labor enjoyed 'a thumping win' that political commentators attributed, at least in part, to the fact that the Liberal–Nationals' 'muscular, conservative law and order agenda' was 'narrow and discordant in a community of progressive sensibility, and one that is defined by complexity and diversity' (Strangio, 2018; also Beaumont, 2018). A 2019 internal Liberal Party report, *2018 Victorian state election review*, conceded that 'the focus on "African gangs" became a distraction for some key voters who saw it as a political tactic rather than an authentic problem to be solved by initiatives that would help make their neighbourhoods safer' (Nutt, 2019, p. 74).

Labor's eventual rebuttal of the explicit racialisation of the 'African gangs' problem in January 2018 seemingly afforded it an opportunity to excuse itself from the law and order auction and instead to campaign on issues that reflected its policy strengths: major transport and infrastructure projects and investments in health and education. Although Labor's victory was also likely influenced by growing disillusionment among moderate Liberal–Nationals voters with the federal Coalition's disarray in Canberra (Economou, 2018), closing what political scientists describe as this 'problem window' (Kingdon, 1984) appears to have been part of an effective election strategy.[5] This is evident from the fact that the percentage of Victorian voters who identified crime as the top issue facing Victoria decreased by 10% between January and September of 2018 in the wake of Dutton's comments (IPSOS, 2018; see Fig. 1.1 in the "Introduction").

It is unclear whether this decrease reflected growing incredulity among voters with respect to the Liberal–Nationals' law and order claims (as suggested by the Liberal Party's own report – see Nutt, 2019), or successful messaging by Labor that:

> Crime has fallen for the fifth quarter in a row, with burglary and break and enter offences the lowest in a decade and the victimisation rate the lowest in 5 years, following the Andrews Labor Government's record community safety investment.
>
> (Neville, 2018)

The irony is that Labor attributed this decrease to the various policies it introduced in response to the Liberal–Nationals' claims of a law and order crisis. Perhaps, in the end, Labor's shoring up of the 'law and order' ground in the lead-up to the 2018 election was due to it having fulfilled the criteria identified in the Liberals' post-election analysis:

> To be successful in Victorian State elections 'law and order' initiatives must be based on, (a) a genuine problem perceived to be relevant to soft voters (who feel a 'personal proximity of a threat'), (b) be addressed with a proportionate and substantive policy solution, and (c) not be perceived by relevant voters as a 'cheap political tactic'.
>
> (Nutt, 2019, p. 74)

Evidently, a progressive government's push towards conservative logic – emphasising community safety, public order, and individual security and responsibility – is more palatable to a pluralist, multicultural public than a conservative party's wild push to gain danger-based legitimacy without a 'substantive policy solution'.

---

[5]The inability of the Greens to effectively capitalise on Labor's concessions to the law and order agenda is also worth acknowledging. This is attributable to a combination of scandals, in-fighting and a poor campaign strategy that ultimately ended up costing the Greens half of their seats to Labor (Willingham, 2019).

Conclusion

Law and order elections are nothing new in Anglophone democracies, and, in many respects, the role that Victorian politicians played in constructing and validating the problems of 'Sudanese thugs' and 'African gangs' was unexceptional. Conservative politicians from the Opposition used the issue to try and present a popular, progressive government as being soft on crime and unwilling to acknowledge the dangers associated with humanitarian migration and resettlement in a prosperous liberal society. From a political standpoint, the strategy was unsuccessful for the reasons discussed above, but the dangerisation of young South Sudanese Australians had a discernible impact on the youth justice policies that were developed by the Andrews government in its efforts to neutralise its opponents' critique. Examining the threat construction process through a political lens thus provides important insight into how South Sudanese Australians in Melbourne came to be identified as a unique threat to community safety following the 2016 Moomba festival and in the lead-up to the 2018 Victorian state election.

At the same time, political analysis alone provides only partial insight into the cultural, economic and social factors that collectively shaped this threat construction process. Indeed, the analysis above suggests that it is impossible to establish a clear demarcation between these different analytical lenses or spheres. In this regard, Koumouris and Blaustein (2021) have argued that, in Victoria and Australia, there appears to exist a symbiotic relationship between some politicians and media institutions. While they encountered only anecdotal and non-verifiable evidence of direct collusion between Liberal politicians and the Murdoch press, their research suggests that the politicisation of the issue, and the policy debates that this gave rise to, provided journalists with a ready supply of newsworthy material. Consistent with Hall et al.'s (1978) adoption of moral panic theory, elements of the media thus seemingly played a crucial role when it came to amplifying the visibility of this problem as a 'secondary definer'.

We further acknowledge the limitations of addressing this question from a purely constructivist perspective. In this regard, we argue that Hall et al.'s (1978) Gramscian approach remains instructive because it reminds us that politicians do not arbitrarily invent problems or threats. Rather, these are constructed by elites in ways that appeal to what they perceive to be established cultural, economic and social anxieties. In this case, the decision to centre a law and order campaign on the 'African gangs crisis' was presumably shaped by politicians' (or their strategists') assumptions about the perceived otherness of South Sudanese Australians within the Victorian community, together with the assumed resonance of this threat construction with established, racialised stereotypes about black and migrant criminality. In this case, the disorder at Moomba offered an ideal political focussing event for reopening a problem window as opposed to constructing a new one (Kingdon, 1984). This occurred at a time when 86% of Australians reportedly held a highly favourable view of multiculturalism (Markus, 2015) and only 28% of prospective Victorian voters identified crime to be one of the three most important issues following Labor's 2014 state electoral victory (see Fig. 1.1 in the "Introduction"; IPSOS, 2015). Put simply, in an increasingly diverse, tolerant and cohesive community, a threat to 'the good society' (Halls-worth & Young, 2008) had to be manufactured and the list of social targets that could fulfil the role of the 'other', the 'stranger', the 'underclass' or 'aliens inside' (Bauman, 2013) was extremely limited.

Chapter 3

The Racialisation of Crime: 'African Gangs' and the Media, with Chloe Keel, Greg Koumouris and Claire Moran

Introduction

A core theme in this book is the racialisation of Sudanese/South Sudanese communities post Moomba and in the lead-up to the 2018 Victorian state election. The previous chapter reflected on the political processes that unfolded across Victoria (and Australia) which helped to position young Sudanese/South Sudanese men as a significant and dangerous threat in the wake of the Moomba 'riot'. We know, however, that this was not the first time that the Sudanese/South Sudanese community in Australia found itself the subject of unwanted attention from politicians and journalists and this is acknowledged by other researchers. For example, Farquharson and Nolan (2018) have examined media representations of Sudanese/South Sudanese people between 2007 and 2012, after the death of Liep Gony and the statements that followed from the then Minister of Immigration, Kevin Andrews. These authors (p. 91) argued that the Minister's comments were not only politically motivated but also 'conditioned by, and resonated within, a news context that had (entirely wrongly) positioned Gony's death as ... endemic to the Sudanese community'. In their subsequent analysis of the media coverage on Sudanese/South Sudanese migrants, perhaps unsurprisingly, they found that news stories pertaining to Sudanese communities were overwhelmingly focussed on crime, with Sudanese/South Sudanese people framed as either perpetrators or victims. More than half of the televised news stories featuring Sudanese/South Sudanese people were focussed on violence. As noted in the Introduction, the Sudanese/South Sudanese community and African Australians more generally have also been a target of conservative columnist Andrew Bolt since at least 2011. Bolt's explicitly racialised and hyperbolic take on the 'problem' is noteworthy in emphasising not only the alleged criminality of African migrants but also the purported inability of humanitarian migrants to integrate successfully and adopt (white) Australian values; the unwillingness of progressive governments to acknowledge this threat and the failure of the multicultural experiment more broadly.

Place, Race and Politics, 41–57

Copyright © 2021 Leanne Weber, Jarrett Blaustein, Kathryn Benier, Rebecca Wickes and Diana Johns

Published under exclusive licence by Emerald Publishing Limited

doi:10.1108/978-1-80043-045-720211003

In this chapter, we examine the media coverage of Sudanese/South Sudanese communities before, during and after the 'crisis'. Drawing on the scholarly literature and a recent study conducted by two of the chapter's authors, we begin by reflecting on various processes and factors which help to account for why stories about 'Sudanese thugs' and 'African gangs' appealed to journalists. The chapter then proceeds to examine the representations of Sudanese/South Sudanese communities during the 'crisis' using a mixed-method media content analysis. Our time series analysis evidences a significant increase in the media's coverage of these issues following Moomba, lasting until the 2018 Victorian state election. This suggests that media outlets were instrumental in co-constructing the threat narrative and provides further evidence of a symbiotic relationship between journalists/editors and politicians. Our thematic analysis evidences that the articles consistently included coded language that both reflected and reproduced narratives emphasising the link between blackness and criminality and the societal risk posed by humanitarian migrants.

Newsworthiness, Race and Crime

Stories about crime typically exhibit multiple characteristics associated with 'newsworthiness', including immediacy, dramatisation, personalisation, simplification, titillation, conventionalism, access and/or novelty (Chibnall, 1977). The newsworthiness of particular incidents, problems or trends may be further enhanced by various factors, such as their scale or visibility; themes of sexuality; the pathological characteristics of the alleged perpetrator(s); a focus on 'worthy' or 'ideal' victims; the immediacy or proximity of the problem, threat or risk and the graphic description of criminal events (Chibnall, 1977). Studies indicate that crimes attributed to racial and ethnic minority perpetrators often receive disproportionately higher attention from traditional media outlets, including newspapers and local television stations (Bjornstrom et al., 2010). Critical scholars argue that this differential coverage often emphasises the racial or ethnic identities of non-white perpetrators, thereby benefiting from and reproducing stereotypical constructions of black or brown criminality (Gilliam et al., 1996; Welch, 2007). In many instances, the racialisation of perpetrators is achieved through the use of coded language, such as 'thugs' or 'packs' (Welch et al., 2004; Windle, 2008), and even 'gangs' (Hallsworth & Young, 2008; Williams, 2015). Racialised crime narratives are pervasive and problematic insofar as they 'erroneously served as a subtle rationale for the unofficial policy and practice of racial profiling by criminal justice practitioners' (Welch, 2007, p. 276). In this way, they contribute to the process of dangerisation by generating a danger-based legitimacy for such practices (Hall et al., 1978; Lianos & Douglas, 2000).

There are various explanations for the differential media representation of perpetrators from racial and ethnic minority groups. Proponents of the power structure approach attribute this to ethnic and racial biases that are said to be embedded within media organisations and reflected in the actions of journalists who act as producers and curators of media content (Bjornstrom et al., 2010,

p. 274; Klein & Naccarato, 2003). Others suggest that newsworthiness is influenced by the market structure of the media sector, with the effect that competition for readership and an increased reliance on advertising revenue create incentives for media outlets to 'produce those stories which they think are of most interest to the public' (Chermak, 1994, p. 561). This implies that news-making practices as a form of cultural production are largely responsive to the values and interests of established and prospective readerships.

It is certainly important to consider the dialectical relationship between media producers and media consumers when it comes to explaining the construction and reproduction of racialised narratives about crime, but we might also question why criminal incidents that are reportedly committed by ethnic minorities remain newsworthy when they are often presented as common or ubiquitous in many media markets (Bjornstrom et al., 2010; Pritchard & Hughes, 1997). Perhaps the answer is that there is actually a scarcity of exceptional crime stories, so seemingly mundane events that can be attributed to a dangerous or pathological perpetrator, although otherwise unexceptional, are still more newsworthy than other local stories.

The appeal of these stories is perhaps further explained by the apparent relative ease with which journalists and television news producers can report on incidents involving violent or property crimes committed by racial and ethnic minorities who for various reasons are at greater risk of coming into contact with the criminal justice system. These stories are also the product of the prohibitive costs associated with investigative reporting (Chermak, 1994). To this effect, Grabosky and Wilson (1989) noted more than 30 years ago that crime reporters were becoming increasingly reliant on police informants to source stories. This practice remains common today, and research by Jones (2021) also suggests that court proceedings provide another source of readily accessible, newsworthy content which reflects, and arguably reproduces, the over-representation of marginalised and over-policed communities within the justice system.

Finally, what is known as the racial threat argument

> ...emphasizes that dominant groups view large minority populations as threatening their advantaged positions ... [and thus] take steps to reduce encroachments on its prerogatives, which results in more pronounced prejudice and discrimination in settings where minority populations are larger.
> (Bjornstrom et al., 2010, p. 275)

In this respect, the racialised crime stories generated by traditional media institutions are argued to reflect and reinforce racial hierarchies and inequalities (Greer & Reiner, 2012). Elements of this perspective clearly resonate with the Gramscian framework adopted by Hall et al. (1978) and with the previous chapter, which concluded by reflecting on the symbiotic relationship between politicians and the media. While the precise motives of individual politicians and media commentators are perhaps diverse, their attempts to frame the 'African gangs' problem as a crisis of multiculturalism certainly indicate that these mobilisers were concerned with preserving their 'advantaged positions'.

Elements of the various theoretical approaches outlined above also resonate with moral panic theory, which has long served as the dominant 'critical' framework for theorising how politicians and media actors contribute to the construction of crime problems and target racialised 'folk devils' in different Anglophone contexts (see, for example, Hawkins, 1995; Keith, 1993; Longazel, 2013; Macek, 2006). Although there are important differences in how key moral panic theorists formulate and apply this concept (see Goode & Ben-Yehuda, 1994), the fundamental idea is that moral panics exist as the product of moral and political entrepreneurship and are then compounded by sensationalist media coverage of a particular issue or problem (Cohen, 1972/2011; Goode & Ben-Yehuda, 1994; Thompson et al., 1998). Moral panics are therefore characterised by an element of distortion and exaggeration with the effect that the social reactions and anxieties that they trigger become markedly disproportionate to the actual severity of the threat or problem (Garland, 2008). Although increasingly scrutinised as a theoretical framework, the 'moral panic' concept remains a staple of the criminological lexicon and has even gained influence beyond academic circles as a 'term regularly used by journalists to describe a process which politicians, commercial promoters and media habitually attempt to incite' (McRobbie & Thornton, 1995, p. 559). As noted by Koumouris and Blaustein (2021), the public utility of this concept was evident from the critical response to the 'African gangs crisis', as various scholars, activists and community members deployed this term to debunk and delegitimise the dominant framing (see Anthony Kelly from the Flemington and Kensington Community Legal Centre, as quoted in Gamlen & Wickes, 2018; Wahlquist, 2018c; Wood, 2017).

The utility of the moral panic framework, when it comes to theorising the construction of the 'African gangs crisis', is questionable. In this regard, Koumouris and Blaustein (2021) note that the journalistic and editorial practices that served to construct and sustain this story were shaped by a complex interplay of cultural factors and the structural conditions of a media sector in crisis. Specifically, the journalists they interviewed emphasised that their coverage of the 'crisis' was shaped by commercial pressures to efficiently generate newsworthy content, along with technological changes that rendered these stories more accessible to reporters and more visible to the public. These pressures were described by journalists working across the sector; however, there was a shared perception among most participants in Koumouris and Blaustein's (2021) study that the *Herald Sun* tabloid had played a leading role in reactivating the 'Apex' story in the aftermath of Moomba. This is attributed to the tabloid's position in the media field, and this positionality influenced journalistic and editorial practices within the outlet. To this effect, participants acknowledged that terms like 'thugs' and 'packs', which critical scholars have elsewhere described as racially coded language, were in fact a staple of crime reporters' vocabulary at the *Herald Sun*.

The study by Koumouris and Blaustein (2021) provides insight into how reporters made sense of, and neutralised, journalistic practices that conflicted with established ethical guidelines. This is important for understanding how and why journalists and media outlets contribute to the production of racialised threat narratives in an increasingly diverse and commercialised media field. Most significantly, from a theoretical standpoint, the research suggests that the explanation in this particular case cannot be reduced to any of the explanatory frameworks described above. Rather, it appears to have been shaped by various factors which collectively, and perhaps unintentionally, served to reactivate a dominant racialised narrative about black/African criminality at a politically opportune moment.

In the next section, we begin our examination of the media's focus on Sudanese/South Sudanese communities and their alleged participation in crime with a time series analysis of the media coverage prior to and after Moomba and prior to and after the 2018 state election period. We then take a closer look at the types of articles that were published during this time to highlight important historical continuities that relate to the framing of this 'problem'.

Sensationalising Moomba in the Media: The Lead-up to the 2018 Victorian State Election

The main goal of the time series analysis is to assess whether trajectories in reporting were significantly different across specific periods of time from 2007, which denotes the beginning of the racialised association between Sudanese/South Sudanese communities and crime, until 2020, when the focus on these communities had significantly lessened. To construct a database of relevant media articles, we identified relevant news publications through electronic searches of bibliographic databases, news pages and Internet search engines. Our inclusion criteria comprised reports in English and those located in mainstream news publications. We did not include articles from regional publications. We initially considered the inclusion of *The Guardian*; however, a review of the articles on the topics of interest to this chapter (noted below) revealed few articles from this source. Thus, our final sample of sources were those that largely targeted a national or Victorian audience. We used Factiva to search the following news sources:

- *Herald Sun*
- *The Age*
- *The Australian*
- *ABC Australia*
- *9NEWS*
- *Daily Telegraph*
- *Sydney Morning Herald* – Australian Breaking News
- *News.com.au* – Australian news site
- *SBS Australia.*

Our search strategy was refined over a number of iterations. A full record of these searches is detailed in Appendix 1. We searched subject headings and text words from 1 January 2007 to 1 December 2020 to capture the initial wave of negative media reporting as identified in Farquharson and Nolan's (2018) research, as well as the media reporting during and post Moomba and leading up to and following the Victorian state election. In order to reduce the number of extraneous search results, we used the following search commands (* was used to capture all words with at least these letters)[1]:

- Gang AND Crime OR

    – Africa*
    – 'South Sudanese'
    – 'South Sudan'
    – Sudan*
    – Apex.

This resulted in 1,479 independent sources, which were all downloaded. Fig. 3.1 illustrates the number of articles per month over the previously stated time period.

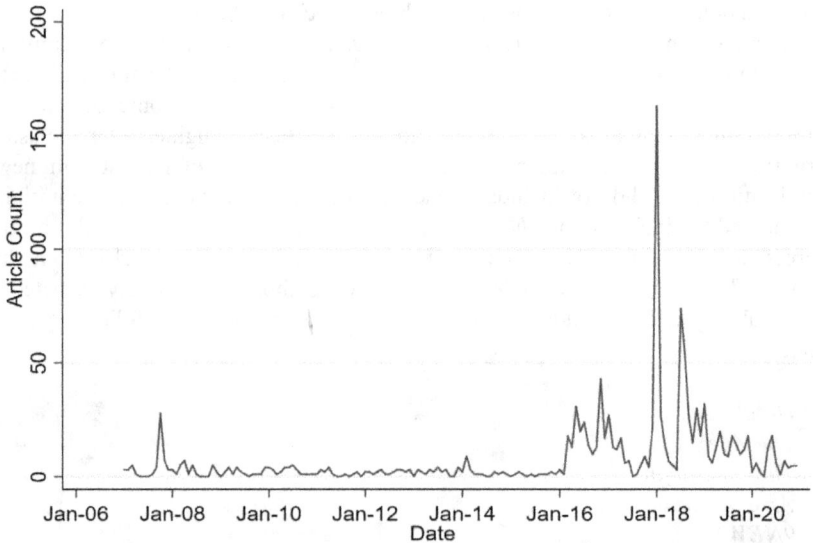

Fig. 3.1.   The Prevalence of Articles Containing the Keywords of Interest per Month.

---

[1]We also included search commands to reduce the number of extraneous articles. These were added after our initial search for the first six keywords when it was evident that many unrelated articles were also captured. These exclusion operators were NOT Bikie, NOT China and NOT Carl Williams.

Fig. 3.1 clearly illustrates a delayed yet significant increase in reporting after the Moomba event. Indeed, after the initial 'shock' of media reporting following Moomba, the trend of articles featuring the aforementioned search terms decreased. We then see a small jump approximately one year after Moomba, followed by a significant increase in media reporting in January 2018, leading up to the Victorian election.

To assess whether there was a significant change in media reporting from what was expected based on the previous trend, we conducted an interrupted time series model to evaluate the impact of two key moments – the Moomba riot and the Victorian state election – on the number of articles on African gangs published in our sample of media outlets.[2] Interrupted time series models are particularly useful for understanding sharp changes in a trajectory and have been widely used to assess the impact of interventions, regulatory actions and critical events on trend data (Linden, 2015).

Fig. 3.2 illustrates the trends in the media reporting relating to our key search terms from 2007 to 2020. The time series regression analyses illustrate that the initial level of media reportage was estimated at 3,343 articles per month, with this trend showing no significant change until the Moomba incident ($B = -0.021$, $p = $ ns). In the same month in which Moomba and the associated disorder took

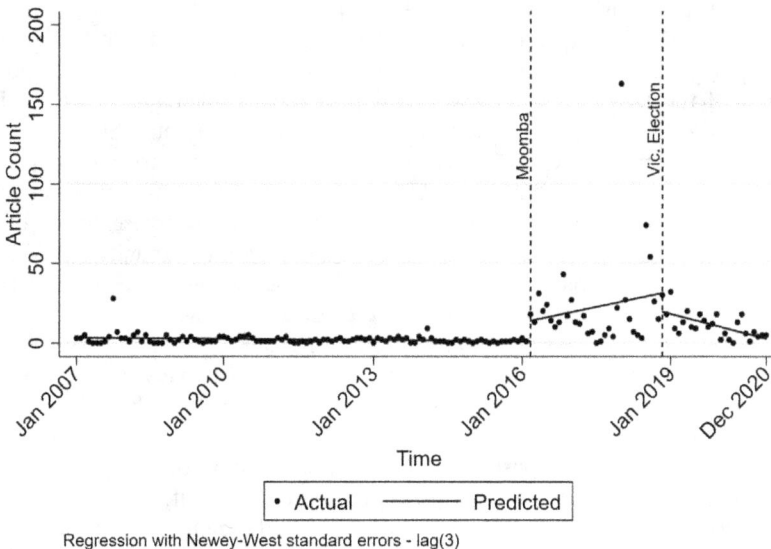

Regression with Newey-West standard errors - lag(3)

Fig. 3.2.   Interrupted Trend Analysis of Media Articles, 2007–2020.

---

[2]Analyses were conducted using the 'itsa' command in Stata 15.

place, the number of articles increased significantly ($B = 12.897$, $p < 0.01$). This trend continued until the Victorian state election held in November 2018. While there was no immediate shift in the number of articles published within the same month of the election ($B = -11.797$, $p =$ ns), following the November 2018 state election, the number of articles began to significantly decrease at a rate of 1,224 articles per month ($p < 0.01$). This decrease continued until the end of the data collection period in December 2020. The time series analysis on the number of articles relating to 'African gangs' after the Moomba incident provides compelling evidence that reporting on this issue was strategically advanced to progress a particular kind of a narrative leading up to the Victorian election. The steep decline following the election serves as further evidence that reporting was not tied to an ongoing problem with Sudanese/South Sudanese communities, but rather, given the loss of the election for the conservative party, that the story was no long appealing or of benefit to the Liberals' platform.

The time series analysis is useful for demonstrating how the reporting trend changed, but it does not provide insights into the actual content of the stories that were circulating in the media at various points during the 'crisis'. For example, the backlash to the law and order rhetoric seemingly peaked in January 2018 and this gave rise to a '#Africangangs' counternarrative disseminated through social media. Following the Liberal Party's claims that Melbourne was in the grip of a 'gang crisis' (see Chapter 2), posts began appearing on Facebook, Twitter and Instagram featuring members of the African community engaging in a range of activities, such as graduating from university, getting married and having children. Lawyers, doctors and other professionals from this community posted photos of themselves at work, contributing to society (Wahlquist, 2018a). This counternarrative was spearheaded by two members of the South Sudanese community, Natalina Andrew and Maker Mayak, and was constructed to demonstrate the everyday contributions of African migrants in Australia and in so doing to speak up against the 'terrorising' effects of the media representation of so-called African gangs for the Sudanese/South Sudanese community (Wahlquist, 2018d). As Koumouris and Blaustein (2021) argue, a point to consider here is that, although these counternarratives are distinct from the dominant construction of these communities and served to challenge the politicised narrative about Melbourne's 'African gangs' problem, they may have also inadvertently served to enhance the visibility and newsworthiness of the story and therefore perhaps extended the news cycle.

Similarly, it must be considered that the politicisation of the 'problem' may have actually been more newsworthy than the problem itself. In essence, a story about crime seemingly gave rise to stories about different law and order (and migration) policy responses, along with stories documenting wider debates about Australian identity, racism and multiculturalism. Supplementing quantitative content analysis with qualitative content analysis is therefore necessary for disentangling these issues and understanding how the 'problem group' was represented in the media during the 'crisis'.

To get a stronger sense of the content of these articles, we conducted a thematic analysis of a sample of the top 100 most relevant articles (as determined by

Factiva). These articles were identified by the prominence and frequency of the search terms in addition to the date of publication. We used the Free Text queries with Boolean logic. This approach looks for the prominence and frequency of the search terms (that is, those words or search terms that appear in the headline or lead paragraph of an article, and the frequency of the word/term's usage). When using multiple terms, as we have done for this search, the proximity of multiple terms is also factored into the article selection. The distribution of the top 100 articles used in the following analyses is roughly in line with the broader search results. However, it is possible that these results are influenced by the search terms, as prominent politicians using these terms fuelled the use of this language in the reporting around youth crime and gangs.

Using NVIVO, we carried out manual coding and focussed on the relational language around being black and being a criminal and on how the settlement and integration of Sudanese/South Sudanese communities was framed. We also coded the articles by their publication date. Again, the time period in which the articles were published was of particular interest to us as we wanted to assess whether and how changes in tone and article content occurred over time and in the lead-up to the Victorian state election. Specifically, we examined tone and content pre Moomba (before 12 March 2016), post Moomba (12 March 2016 to November 2017), in the year prior to the Victorian election (December 2017 to 24 November 2018) and in the period following the election (from 25 November 2018 onwards) (see Table 3.1). We also considered whether tone and content differed across the different media outlets (see Table 3.2). We know from other research (see Chapter 5) that alignment with a more conservative political party resulted in greater anger and less warmth towards migrants of colour, particularly migrants from Africa or who endorsed the Muslim faith (Wickes et al., 2020). Thus, we were particularly interested to establish whether outlets with a conservative bias that reflected their readership were more likely to frame crime attributed to Sudanese/South Sudanese communities as a problem.[3]

Our media analysis also revealed distinct time frames during which both the number of articles increased and the framing of 'Africans' as a problem became more overt. As with the larger sample, our content analysis found that the majority of articles were concentrated in the period prior to the Victorian election (72 articles), followed by those that appeared post Moomba (17 articles). It is worth noting that of these 100 articles analysed, many were not tied to a specific and/or notorious crime event. Instead, these articles were focussed on comments made by politicians, police and public figures. Once again this speaks to the idea that it is difficult, perhaps impossible, to disentangle political and media influences when it comes to analysing the construction of a 'law and order crisis'; the election increased the newsworthiness of incidents that fit with the 'crisis' narrative and media coverage of the incidents served to evidence the problem and

---

[3]This was indeed the perception of journalists who reported on these issues during the 'crisis', with one participant in Koumouris and Blaustein's (2021) study suggesting that in the case of the *Herald Sun*, this partly reflected the paper's victim-centric focus when it came to presenting crime stories.

Table 3.1. Top 100 Most Relevant Articles by Time Period.

Period of Time	Number of Articles in Top 100
Pre Moomba (before 12 March 2016)	1
Post Moomba (on and after 12 March 2016 until November 2017)	17
Pre Victorian election (December 2017 to 24 November 2018)	72
Post Victorian election (after 24 November 2018)	10

validate political narratives that located responsibility with the South Sudanese community.

Overall, the print coverage of South Sudanese or Sudanese people centred on violence, as was evidenced in the earlier work of Nolan and colleagues (2014). Immigration-related discourses were also present and centred on the challenges faced by these communities or their failure or inability to 'integrate'. Notions of blackness and its intersection with criminality were signalled throughout the publications to differing degrees, depending on the political positioning of the media outlet. We discuss these themes in more detail below.

The Emergence of the 'Law and Order Crisis'

The most relevant 100 articles derived by Factiva followed a very similar temporal pattern to that found in the time series analysis. Approximately 65% of references to 'Apex' within the 100 most relevant articles occurred in the post-Moomba period. Across these articles, only two publications, *The Age* and *ABC*

Table 3.2. Top 100 Most Relevant Articles by Media Outlet.

Publication	Number of Articles in Top 100
Herald Sun	12
The Age	22
The Australian	42
ABC Australia	21
9NEWS	0
Daily Telegraph	2
SMH – Australian Breaking News	0
News.com.au – Australian news site	1
SBS Australia	0

online, reported on Victoria Police's statement that the Apex gang was a non-entity or that it was essentially a group of Australian-born offenders comprising 'a mixture of numerous ethnicities, [and] nationalities' (*The Age*, April 2017). In contrast, other articles framed 'Apex' as a problem specific to the African community in Melbourne, with a particular focus on Sudanese Australians. A South Sudanese community leader, Richard Deng, is quoted in the *Sunday Age* as arguing that the media coverage led to a common perception that 'All the kids that are African are Apex' (Mills & Hall, 2017).

In the height of the era of misinformation and 'fake news', despite low crime rates and Victoria Police stating that the group 'never was predominately African' (*ABC News*, April 2017), the myth of the African gang in Melbourne was pervasive. Consequently, the law and order discussion did not revolve around deviant youth in the community, but specifically around 'Sudanese' and 'African' youth, who became a significant feature in the political discourse leading up to the 2018 Victorian election (see Chapter 2).

The 2018 Victorian state election saw a resurgence of interest in 'African gangs', with 72 out of the 100 articles in our content analysis published within the period from December 2017 to the election on 24 November 2018. Once again, the most prominent articles published in the lead-up to the Victorian election were not driven by highly publicised crime events, but rather by the comments of federal politicians and commentators. In the lead-up to the election, media articles were framed around whether or not Victoria was in the middle of an African gang problem, and cited in these articles were a number of claims from senior Liberal/National party members. It is our contention that these claims were deeply political and out of step with both the Victorian Government's and Victoria Police's official positions.

Of the Factiva top 100 most relevant articles examined, 49 articles referenced at least one such claims. The harm that these sensationalised accounts caused is discussed further in Chapter 5. Referring to the family of Liep Gony, the young man murdered in Noble Park, Melanie Poole of the Federation of Community Legal Centres commented in *The Australian* that:

> If anything, this surge in media coverage ... and comments by the likes of Scott Morrison, Malcolm Turnbull, Peter Dutton, Matthew ... have re-traumatised them.
>
> (*The Australian*, September 2018)

The tone of the coverage was largely driven by the source of the articles – for example, *The Australian* was more emotive, while *The Age* and the *ABC* attempted to present a more balanced perspective. Based on our analyses of the most relevant 100 articles, *The Age* and the *ABC* stopped repeating the political posturing that marked the beginning of the 2018 Victorian election period. In contrast, media outlets like *The Australian* continued to refer to the comments made by coalition leaders for a much longer period, and these comments were used to support opinion pieces in lieu of new events or public comments. An article by Rachel Baxendale on 23 July serves as a case in point. In this article,

Baxendale leads with comments about African crime made previously by Liberal Ministers Alan Tudge and Peter Dutton (Baxendale, 2018).

Our analyses also revealed that key commentators drove the discourse on each side. It was largely the federal Liberals who led with more aggressive claims against the African communities, particularly in the lead-up to the Victorian election. Key South Sudanese leaders ran a counternarrative. Richard Deng, a South Sudanese community leader, is quoted or referenced in 14 of the 100 articles in the analysis. The positioning of narrative in these articles demonstrates a familiar pattern: politicians encouraging a fear of blackness as a foundational marker of their law and order campaign, which is then countered by a strong campaign from the targeted community – in this case the South Sudanese community – to refute problematic evidence and reject harmful and largely inaccurate stereotypes.

The language used to describe offenders and offences also differed across the articles we reviewed. Articles that took a more sympathetic position would often refer to 'youth crime' and if country of origin was mentioned they would refer to 'African Australians' or 'South Sudanese youth'. Articles that took a more critical position would use terms such as 'gang', 'thugs', 'crisis' or 'crime wave' – terms that incite a sense of panic and fear and conjure images of an uncontrollable group of youths 'terrorising' particular places. In line with the work of Cunneen (2020), in these articles, risk is linked (sometimes implicitly, sometimes explicitly) with blackness and cultural difference, both of which are constructed as 'dangerous'. In this vein, conservative commentators and politicians called for the 'gangs' to be called for 'what they were'. They argued that refusing to use the word 'gang' was further evidence that the current Labor government was 'soft on crime'. In some of these articles, the framing of the issue in other states was used to highlight the 'soft' approach of both the Victorian Government and Victoria Police. For example, New South Wales Police embraced the use of the word 'gang' and criticised Victoria Police for being unwilling to acknowledge the 'ethnic' dimension of the problem:

> New South Wales Police on Wednesday said they are not afraid to identify a group of youths responsible for a crime spree targeting electronic stores across Sydney as an 'African gang'. Unlike Melbourne police, who got themselves tongue-tied trying to avoid using the words 'African' and 'gang' despite the obvious ethnic violence on their streets, NSW Assistant Commissioner Mark Jones said: 'We will call it for what it is'.
>
> (Fife-Yeomans, 2019)

As evidenced in our time series analysis, there was a significant drop in reporting on 'African gangs' after the 2018 Victorian election. Only 10 of the 100 most relevant articles analysed in the content analysis were published after the election (Delibasic & Travers, 2020; Fife-Yeomans, 2019; Herald Sun, 2019; Martin, 2018; Simonis et al., 2020a, 2020b; Smith, 2019; The Australian, 2018; Visentin, 2018). These articles received less commentary from public figures and were largely related to actual crimes that had occurred. Most notable was the fatal stabbing of

Solomone Taufeulungaki in Deer Park, Victoria, in 2019. Of interest here is that although there was no direct link between Sudanese/South Sudanese young people and this attack, as was reported in the media, the incident nonetheless provided the stimulus for additional commentary on the state of the 'African gang' problem in Victoria or the hostile relationships between Pasifika and South Sudanese 'gangs' (Herald Sun, 2019). This suggests that, even after the election, narratives about 'African gangs' remained newsworthy, albeit to a lesser degree.

Blackness and Criminality

A key theme emerging from the articles we reviewed was the association between blackness and criminality. As we argue in the introductory chapter, and indeed throughout the book, blackness is more than skin colour, it is socially constructed in opposition to whiteness (Mapedzahama & Kwansah-Aidoo, 2017). Across countries and time, the black body is categorised as the criminal 'other' and those who are black are pushed to the 'margins of society' (Mapedzahama & Kwansah-Aidoo, 2017; see also Fanon, 1986). In Australia, the paradox of the burden of blackness is simultaneous hypervisibility and invisibility (Mapedzahama & Kwansah-Aidoo, 2017). African migrants are viewed as 'too dark, too tall, speaking too many languages, too culturally diverse and belonging to too many places' (Ndhlovu, 2014, p. 129). Their distinctive physical characteristics make African migrants easy targets as 'foreigners' or 'strangers' by the broader Australian community (Hatoss, 2012). At the same time, the black body is invisible in everyday life. Studies demonstrate this invisibility in doctors' offices (Kamaloni, 2019), in retail stores (Mapedzahama & Kwansah-Aidoo, 2013) and in a lack of everyday representations in the media (Ndhlovu, 2014). Noble (2005) argues that invisibility is the active regulation of the unfit existence of others. Here, the other is not seen as a 'legitimate part' of society.

As hypervisible migrants, black Africans are perceived as 'perpetual suspects' (Long, 2018) who are subject to racial profiling and police targeting. There is substantial evidence in the academic literature that the concept of 'gang' is disproportionately applied to black and Asian minorities. Williams and Clarke (2016, p. 10) argue that 'the gang construct is racialised to Black and Brown men'. The successful application of this label shapes policing and justifies then police use of force against people of colour (Long, 2018). In a study on African Australian men, Majavu (2017) found that white perpetrators used perceptions of Africans as violent gang members to justify violence against them. Participant Kenny stated,

> After midnight I was going home … I see this white guy coming towards me … I was trying to move out of his way, but he blocked me … He says to me "You think you're a gangster, huh?".
>
> (p. 51)

The media articles that we have examined use language pertaining to youth crime that signifies blackness as the culprit. While the framing of youth crime varied across articles, references to coded signifiers of blackness and otherness were pervasive. Articles consistently referred to 'Africa' or 'Sudan' and asked South Sudanese community leaders to comment. Even the more reasoned articles positioned race as central to understanding youth crime. A large proportion of the articles in the 100 most relevant Factiva list positioned Africans/South Sudanese as perpetrators of violent crime.

> It's not news that Sudanese-Australians are over-represented in crime figures but until now, the spread and scale of the problem has not been put clearly on the map.
>
> (*The Australian*, November 2018)

> One would have thought a mob of African males invading a home and punching a woman in the face might make multiculturalists repent. Perhaps a mob of African males attacking teens on the street might stir Melbourne's green-left to unmitigated sympathy – for the victims.
>
> (*The Australian*, January 2018)

Among those articles that considered the factors that may lead South Sudanese youth into crime, the 'victim of circumstance' argument was raised, still positioning such youth as a danger or a problem group, destined for deviance and incapable of assimilating due to their lax parenting, cultural differences or traumatic pasts.

> 'Kids are growing with very little structure within families, many of them don't have male figures in their families', he said. 'Child protection laws are actually fuelling this crisis. There has got to be some understanding of the cultural background of people. In most African families, the rearing of the children is a little on the tough side rather than being very permissive...'.
>
> (*The Australian*, July 2016)

By positioning Sudanese/South Sudanese youth as 'broken people' who come 'from war zones', such articles mention the deficits of these experiences and say nothing about the incredible resilience of migrants who survive such circumstances to build a better life in a new country. Instead, even in the articles that highlighted the trauma faced by the Sudanese/South Sudanese community, there was an assumption that this particular migrant community had a predisposition towards crime because of such experiences.

A Failure to Settle Well

As Katje Franko (2020) contends, labelling particular groups of migrants as crimmigrants is a way to transform them into a group that should be justifiably excluded and, if not deported, at a minimum should be subjected to surveillance and punishment. We see this play out in the analyses of the articles reviewed for this chapter. More conservative publications such as *The Australian* directly linked discussions of 'African youth crime' to debates around migration. Imagery of the *criminal migrant* was apparent across many articles, while opinion pieces explicitly created a link between youth crime and anti-immigration.

> The spectre of Apex came to prominence at the Moomba riots in 2016, when youths ran amok in the CBD and thrust the idea of migrant crime to the forefront.
>
> (*ABC News*, April 2017)

> Liberal democratic societies are expected to turn a blind eye to any problematic cultural behaviour they bring with them, especially if the immigrants have brown skin.
>
> (*The Australian*, July 2018)

Additionally, the dangerisation of the African community – their transformation into a group that represents danger and risk – was overlaid with references to Labor government leaders who were more in favour of migration in general. This was evidenced most clearly in Bernard Lane's article in *The Australian* that appeared on 19 November 2018, just days before the Victorian election, in which he linked the location of the crime to Labor federal and state leaders:

> Bill Shorten's federal seat of Maribyrnong in the city's northwest overlaps with the LGA of the same name, which has the biggest share of African-born crime in relation to total crime. Premier Daniel Andrews' own district of Mulgrave, in the east, intersects with the LGA that has the second highest share of African crime.
>
> (*The Australian*, November 2018)

Other articles discussed African migrants' integration and settlement and their association with crime.

> Yet even harder to discuss than speed of migration is the identity of migrants. But identity matters, because – and here is a great shibboleth to break – some identities are simply easier to integrate than others. There are 67 suburbs in Melbourne and Sydney in which more than half of the residents were born overseas.
>
> (*The Australian*, March 2018)

What was particularly striking in many of the articles was the relative lack of reflection or discussion on the role played by those who are already settled in the welcome and reception of new migrant groups. Certainly, we know from the literature that increasing ethno-racial diversity can be viewed as highly disruptive and threatening to the settled community. Yet, with the recent rise of 'threat narratives' (Vertovec, 2017) and the 'politics of fear' (Massey, 2015) around migration, the association of highly visible new migrants with threat narratives about African migrants in general has the potential to turn a particular event or issue into a discourse of crisis. This 'crisis', in turn, can lead to proposals in legislation specifically designed to exclude migration or particular groups from migrating. We saw this in 2007 and 2008, when then Federal Immigration Minister Kevin Andrews reduced the number of Sudanese/South Sudanese migrants who could apply for residency in Australia. In the aftermath of Moomba, a push for more exclusionary migration policies was also evident in a proposed amendment to the *Migration Act 1958* which, if adopted, would have enhanced Ministerial discretion around the cancellation of the visas of non-citizens on character grounds, including potentially children and first-time offenders (see Powell & Martin, 2018). Positioning one's 'failure to settle' as something attributable only to those who are building a new life in Australia masks the barriers to settlement that are beyond the migrant's control.

Concluding Thoughts

In their edited book *Australian Media and the Politics of Belonging*, Nolan et al. (2018) brought together a group of scholars to examine how media texts represent or construct belonging or exclusion for particular migrant groups. As part of this work, Farquharson and Nolan (2018) focussed on the media representation of Sudanese/South Sudanese people in Australia from 2007 to 2012, a period that marked the initial onslaught of media attention on these communities following Liep Gony's death. In their analysis of the media coverage on Sudanese/South Sudanese migrants, these authors found news stories pertaining to Sudanese communities to be overwhelmingly focussed on crime, with Sudanese/South Sudanese people framed as either perpetrators or victims. Their research also revealed that more than half of televised news stories that featured Sudanese/South Sudanese people focussed on violence. In this chapter we took a deeper look at the media coverage of Sudanese communities from 2007 to 2020 with the specific goal of identifying whether or not the overall trend was for media reporting to escalate during this period as a result of the Moomba incident and how media coverage on 'African gangs' was amplified in the lead-up to the 2018 Victorian state election.

Our findings are not qualitatively different from those of Farquharson and Nolan's (2018) initial qualitative research. The time series analyses conducted in our study tell a compelling story. We can see from the results of these analyses that the number of news articles began to increase in the immediate aftermath of Moomba in 2016 and that this increase was significantly different from earlier periods. Yet our findings also show that the number of articles about the Sudanese/South Sudanese community only reached their peak in January 2018 – at this point there were three times more articles published than immediately following Moomba. Further evidence that the Australian media constructs narratives of belonging that are deeply politicised and at times racialised is found in the significant and swift decline in the amount of media reporting on Sudanese/ South Sudanese communities following the 2018 Victorian election, when the Labor Party was returned to government.

The tone and content of the articles we qualitatively examined revealed that the usual tropes that position people of colour as the deviant other were present, as were the claims that some migrant groups are more prone to criminality than others and thus fail to successfully integrate into their host country. As we note in our Introduction and demonstrate further in Chapter 5, this escalation of the crimmigrant narrative (Franko, 2020) was not without consequence. The findings from research by Wickes and colleagues (2020) and Benier et al. (2020) demonstrate the strong association between the 'African gangs' media coverage and anti-African sentiments in Melbourne following the Moomba incident. In a randomised survey of Melbourne residents undertaken late in 2017, nearly one in six participants reported anger towards Africans and one in four participants reported low levels of warmth towards Africans (Wickes et al., 2020). Though we are not proposing that there is a direct, causal relationship between media reporting and sentiments towards migrants, the evidence from our media analysis does suggest that the reporting on 'African gangs' likely contributed to these harmful sentiments. Reflecting on the IPSOS data (see Fig. 1.1 in Introduction), there also appears to be a clear correlation between the media's coverage of the 'crisis' and growing public concerns about crime as an electoral issue.

The consistent focus on the alleged offending of a small number of young people from Sudanese/South Sudanese communities serves only to strengthen an underlying bias already present in Australia. Australian media has associated blackness, both African and Indigenous, with problems of crime and delinquency in this country (Majavu, 2020; Mapedzahama & Kwansah-Aidoo, 2017). This inclination to perceive this association, combined with extensive and damaging media and political rhetoric, has led to increasing hostilities towards Sudanese/ South Sudanese communities across various time points since they arrived in Australia in the early 2000s. The racialised crime narratives that took hold after Liep Gony's brutal murder and then again following the Moomba incidents in 2016 demonstrate a pervasive and problematic association between blackness and crime that can be readily accessed and heightened for purposes that may have little to do with reducing crime or indeed highlighting a crime problem of particular significance, when considered against the total crime in a given area or time period. This continued association constitutes a process of dangerisation (Lianos & Douglas, 2000), particularly for migrants from African communities. This is clearly evidenced in the news articles we reviewed and the justifications they presented for limiting migration and increasing police presence in particular communities. The media positioning of offending as a problem unique to particular groups establishes these groups' offending risk as different from that of the rest of society and constructs them as more unpredictable and dangerous. The racialisation of crime narratives and the distinctly constructed discourses of risk, danger and safety in media reports are associated with an increase in social exclusion for Sudanese/South Sudanese communities, as we discuss throughout this book.

Chapter 4

'No-one Thinks You Are Innocent': Policing the 'Crimmigrant Other'

Victoria Police and the 'African Crime' Crisis

The analysis in the previous chapters showed that the media-fuelled law and order crisis around African youth crime continued to reverberate for some time after the disturbances at the 2016 Moomba Festival, rising to a crescendo just before the 2018 Victorian state election. In January 2018, as hostile media reporting about 'African crime' reached fever pitch, the Chief Commissioner of Victoria Police, no doubt under political pressure to act, responded by establishing an African Australian Community Task Force which included police and community membership (Florance, 2018). As mentioned in earlier chapters, its role was to provide information about emerging issues and trends to senior levels within Victoria Police in order to stem 'African crime', yet it remained relatively disconnected from day-to-day police operations at the local level. While the intention of police managers may have been to cool the media debate by being seen to 'do something', the very existence of a high-profile taskforce specifically targeting this sector of the community simultaneously reinforced the view that African Australians did pose a unique threat to other residents and were themselves responsible for finding a solution to the supposed crisis. Moreover, as Windle (2008, p. 563) noted in relation to similar police initiatives introduced at earlier stages of the 'crisis', focussing on improved communication 'cast[s] misunderstanding and miscommunication rather than racism as the source of problems'.

Police Commissioner at the time, Graham Ashton, used the opportunity provided by the taskforce launch to dismiss allegations made by federal politicians that Victoria was unsafe or in crisis and questioned the use of the term 'African gangs', which he said gave a false impression of highly organised groups of young offenders. Instead, he identified the problem as one of an increasing incidence of acts of public disorder committed by groups of young people and preferred the only slightly more nuanced term of 'street gang behaviour' (Windle, 2008, p. 563).

In an apparent attempt to acknowledge African Australians also as potential victims, rather than solely as offenders, the taskforce was mandated to report on instances of racial vilification. No acknowledgement was ever made that frontline

Place, Race and Politics, 59–87
Copyright © 2021 Leanne Weber, Jarrett Blaustein, Kathryn Benier, Rebecca Wickes and Diana Johns
Published under exclusive licence by Emerald Publishing Limited
doi:10.1108/978-1-80043-045-720211004

police practices themselves – discussed later in this chapter – could at times represent a form of racial vilification or worse. Moreover, media coverage of the taskforce launch suggests that this term of reference was envisaged more as a protective measure for community leaders participating in the programme than as a broader recognition of the serious and widespread racism experienced by African Australians (Florance, 2018; SBS News, 2018).

In fact, racism in the policing of African Australian youths had come under the spotlight in Victoria several years earlier, when the *Haile-Michael* case (mentioned in the opening chapter) was brought under the Commonwealth Racial Discrimination Act by the Flemington and Kensington Community Legal Centre and others. That litigation, which was decided in the Federal Court in 2013 via a settlement with Victoria Police, established that discriminatory policing had occurred in the inner western suburbs of Melbourne through repeated and unjustified street stops targeting African Australian youths.[1] The Court accepted statistical evidence provided by an expert witness which showed that young people of African descent were disproportionately stopped by police in those suburbs by a factor of 2.5. The ramifications of the finding were felt across the entire metropolitan area, as Victoria Police undertook fundamental revisions to its cultural awareness training and field contact policies with the intention of eradicating both individual racism and 'racial profiling',[2] a systemic practice the existence of which had not been acknowledged until then within senior police ranks (Kelly, 2015). Changes were introduced to the police manual including a new definition of racial profiling as 'making policing decisions that are not based on objective or reasonable justification, but on stereotypical assumptions about race, colour, language, ethnicity, ancestry or religion' (Police Accountability Project, n.d.). The new instructions also stressed that officers were required to consider the legal basis for conducting street stops (Green, 2015), a fundamental tenet of democratic policing that seemingly had not hitherto been front of mind for operational police.

However, research into police occupational culture has established that 'mission statements' promulgated by senior management will not necessarily change operational practice, unless other influences such as law and policy, public expectations and systemic practices and understandings embedded in rank-and-file culture are all aligned in support of change (Chan, 1997). The Flemington and Kensington Community Legal Centre continued to monitor the implementation of the police undertakings through its Police Accountability Project,[3] producing several reports that questioned the extent to which changes in police training and policy had flowed through to practices on the ground. Two of the *Haile-Michael* complainants authored a report in 2015 entitled *The more things change, the more they stay the same*, which asserted that over-policing of African communities was continuing

---

[1] *Haile-Michael v Konstantinidis* [2012] FCA 108, [2012] FCA 167, [2013] FCA 53.
[2] Racial profiling, although a commonly used term, tends to create the impression that it only occurs when race is explicitly flagged in operational policies, a mistaken view that may be one reason that these practices are resistant to change.
[3] http://www.policeaccountability.org.au/.

across several sites, including Dandenong, a suburb in south-eastern Melbourne that was not covered in the original litigation (Haile-Michael & Issa, 2015).

Katja Franko (2020) has noted that 'crimmigrant others' are not constructed solely through discursive means, but also through multiple exclusionary practices, many of which remain unseen. In this chapter we relate how police in one area of Melbourne both responded and contributed to the construction of young African Australians as crimmigrant others, including through the use of risk-based technologies, and identify their pivotal role in shaping a wider 'politics of belonging' (Yuval-Davis, 2011). We draw on data from an empirical study conducted in the south-eastern suburbs of Melbourne from 2017 to 2018, at the height of the pre-election media frenzy surrounding 'African crime'. The research involved focus groups and interviews with young people and some older community members from Pasifika and South Sudanese Australian backgrounds about their experiences with local police (fully reported in Weber, 2018, 2020a).[4]

In total, 79 people participated formally in the study. In addition, multiple informal discussions took place between the researcher and local youth and community workers. The first phase involved discussions with overseas-born young people from a variety of backgrounds about their experiences of belonging. A second phase included four focus groups involving 33 young people (13 female, 20 male) and three interviews with 5 young people (all male) of Pasifika and South Sudanese heritage who had experienced contact with police, some of them on multiple occasions. In addition, five group interviews were conducted in that phase with 19 adults who were community workers and/or community-engaged parents from Pasifika or South Sudanese backgrounds.[5] We focus here on the reported experiences of the South Sudanese Australian participants in that study and the additional insights into local policing practice provided through our discussions with local youth workers and Victoria Police members.[6,7]

Data collection for this study spanned two culturally diverse local government areas served by a single Division of Victoria Police. The City of Greater Dandenong is a longstanding hub of settlement for refugees, with a reputation for welcoming diverse populations, and has relatively well-established local services for asylum seekers and migrants. According to the latest census, 64% of residents

---

[4]This self-description is widely used in Australia by people of Pacific Islander heritage and Indigenous Māori from New Zealand/Aotearoa.

[5]The researcher thanks members of the Pasifika and South Sudanese Australian communities who assisted with recruitment of research participants and remained engaged with the research throughout. The project culminated in the establishment of SEPIN, the South East Policing and Inclusion Network.

[6]The term South Sudanese Australians is used in this chapter because most of the African Australian participants were recruited through a community group identifying as 'South Sudanese'. The word 'Australian' is applied for reasons of inclusiveness and does not necessarily imply that all participants had legal citizenship in Australia.

[7]The authors wish to acknowledge the cooperation of Victoria Police in this aspect of the study.

of this local government area were born overseas, nearly double the national average.[8] With rising property prices in the area, youth workers advised that many of the communities likely to have the most contact with police had moved further out to the City of Casey. That area is slightly less diverse, with 44% of residents born outside Australia – still well above the national average of 33%.[9] Between them these adjacent local government areas account for the highest proportion of overseas-born residents (Dandenong) and the highest absolute number of overseas-born residents (Casey) in the state of Victoria (Department of Premier and Cabinet, 2017, p. 4).

Although they are far from the most numerous cultural minorities in the study area, South Sudanese and Pasifika young people emerged as the most likely groups to have contact with police. Young people of these backgrounds were also frequently associated with the so-called Apex gang that was said to have its base in Dandenong. As noted in previous chapters, the Apex gang had been implicated in media reporting, particularly concerning the Moomba disturbances, despite repeated public statements by Victoria Police that the young people involved in those events were generally not members of established gangs and came from a range of cultural and linguistic backgrounds (Zielinski & Booker, 2016). In fact, the senior echelons of Victoria Police had been described by one prominent commentator during the height of the media frenzy around Moomba as 'the sanest voice in this African gangs thing' (Wahlquist, 2018d).

However, the extent to which police practice at the local level aligned with these public statements is open to question. In contrast with the intense focus in Flemington and Kensington on the policing of communities originating largely from the Horn of Africa, there has been very little research on encounters between police and African youths in the Dandenong area. The *Boys, you wanna give me some action?* report, which predated the crescendo of the racialised law and order crisis by several years, documented the experiences of African youths across three locations in Melbourne, including Dandenong. The experiences reported by young people in that publication included being treated as outsiders in their communities and being harassed, 'wound up' and treated violently by police (Smith & Reside, 2010).

Greater Dandenong was selected as the site for our study partly because of its connection to the Apex gang narrative, but mainly due to the relative lack of information about the policing of African Australian youths in that part of Melbourne. Indeed, in the initial stages of fieldwork in late 2016, some local government officials advised that little of interest would be identified through the research. Dandenong, they claimed, was not like Flemington. The area was known for its proactive police-led programmes aimed at preventing youth offending, had a small but active team of specialist youth and community liaison officers and was considered by these local actors to have put to rest any conflict

[8]http://quickstats.censusdata.abs.gov.au/census_services/getproduct/census/2016/quickstat/LGA22670.
[9]http://quickstats.censusdata.abs.gov.au/census_services/getproduct/census/2016/quickstat/LGA21610.

between police and young people that may have occurred in the past. But the perception that there were no problems related to the policing of African youth turned out to be far from accurate, and it did not take long to uncover extensive reports from local South Sudanese Australian residents about unexplained and sometimes hostile police stops, discriminatory targeting, serious racial vilification and racist violence. In fact, the picture that emerged from the study confirmed Franko's (2020) claim that individuals and groups that had been socially designated as 'crimmigrant others' were liable to increased surveillance, the application of penal power and – ultimately – physical exclusion.

Securitising Race and Place

Young People as Risk

While police in Dandenong used a variety of approaches, both proactive and reactive, to deal with youth offending, it was their risk-based approach – often associated with paradigms of security and securitisation – that aligned most closely with the experiences reported by community members. A local senior police officer advised the researchers that around 5,000 youths had been charged across the Division during 2015–16, for offences relating mainly to stolen cars, street robbery and break-ins. The emotionally charged offence of 'home invasion' which attracted significant media coverage in relation to 'African crime' was not specifically mentioned. The policing approach in the Division was said to have three strands: a proactive and disruptive approach, particularly towards youth crime; 'a little bit of rehabilitation' through referrals and collaborative working with other agencies and a standard 'response type model'. Having been tasked with 'stemming the tide' of what the media repeatedly referred to as 'Apex gang offending', the police, this officer explained, viewed the problem in terms of looser groupings of young people they labelled 'youth network offenders'. He explained: 'The thing is, it's not *West Side Story* we're dealing with. We're dealing with social media that connects all the youth together'.

The 'proactive' and 'disruptive' strand of the policing of young people in this area is underpinned by a technology-enabled risk-based system. The increasing reliance on automated risk-based systems has been noted in relation to many areas of governance, including policing (Haggerty & Ericson, 2000; O'Malley, 2010). For some time now intelligence-led techniques, often employing predictive algorithms to estimate risks of future offending, have provided a powerful tool to police around the world for targeting resources at people and places designated as 'high risk'. These approaches have been considered successful within some contexts, for example, in understanding the risks posed to children in family violence situations (see, for example, Fitz-Gibbon et al., 2019). However, different considerations come into play in the context of street policing, where encounters are often initiated by police and largely involve young people. A recent review of a risk-based system used by New South Wales Police – the Suspect Targeting Management Plan – concluded that risk-based methods should not be used at all in relation to young people because they are racially discriminatory in practice, result in early contact of young people with police and encourage police interventions for which there is no legal basis (Sentas & Pandolfini, 2017).

The risk-based system used by Victoria Police classifies certain young people who have been in conflict with the law as either 'youth network offenders' – abbreviated to 'YNOs' – or 'core youth network offenders'. These designations are based primarily on age and the number and type of previous offences recorded on police systems. A local inspector explained:

> We can run that tool now and it will tell us – like the kid might be 15 – it tells how many crimes he is going to commit before he is 21 based on that, and it is a 95% accuracy. It has been tested.

This statement reflects both a high level of confidence in the reliability of the predictive tool and a readiness to assign young people into clearly defined categories of low and high risk.

A wider range of data, including family violence and school records, missing persons reports and field contacts, is deployed in a separate predictive tool that is used to identify young people considered to be at risk of future offending. Because these young people are not yet captured within crime statistics, police-initiated field contacts are relied on heavily within this system to provide the necessary data. As the same officer explained: 'They might not have committed a crime but they have been checked at midnight a couple of times, out with other kids'. While 'at-risk' young people would be referred for 'early intervention' support provided by service agencies, aimed at preventing their entry into the criminal justice system, young people identified as YNOs, particularly those classified as core YNOs, were said to be likely to receive intensive monitoring and policing responses. Although one local officer claimed that gangs, as usually understood, were not a significant problem in the area, a group of core YNOs were nevertheless identified as representing an ongoing threat to the security of the wider community.

Tasking to particular locations was also said to be intelligence-led, but was perceived by local police officers as problem-focussed, and not linked in any ongoing way to particular places or categories of people. Officers might also attend locations in a reactive manner, such as shopping centres or public parks where young people were gathering, in response to calls from members of the public. Here, the issue was said to be around 'balancing the tension between allowing youth to be youth' and meeting community expectations. At other times, police might target particular places proactively, using move-on powers, for example, to break up groups of young people gathering to drink alcohol in order to pre-empt serious crimes such as rapes and robberies, which they said had occurred in those circumstances. While local police downplayed the role of place in shaping risk calculations, Protective Services Officers (PSOs) – who have been authorised in Victoria to exercise police powers only in designated areas surrounding train stations – were regularly deployed in the Dandenong area and encouraged to 'engage' with young people.[10] In this case, the notion that train stations are inherently risky places had been explicitly built into their role, with proactive policing intervention actively encouraged in order to transform train stations into securitised spaces.

While the purpose of our study was not to evaluate particular policing pro-grammes, the patterns of police encounters reported by community members aligned remarkably closely with the risk-based approaches described by police. Young people encountered these systems in three clearly identifiable contexts: when they were classified by police as 'high risk' due to past offending and subjected to ongoing monitoring; when they experienced intrusive and unex-plained stops in the absence of either current or past offending and when they were approached, questioned and moved on by police when gathering in public places.

Cleanskins and Criminals

Without knowing the specifics of the risk-based system used by police, local youth workers who supported young people who came into conflict with the law observed that police tended to place young people into rigid categories of either 'cleanskin' or 'criminal'. These workers claimed that intensive policing of young people deemed to be 'criminals' (equating to the categories of YNOs or core YNOs) often undermined the genuine efforts made by these young people to change their lives. Young South Sudanese Australians in our study who disclosed that they had been in conflict with the law reported being forever judged on the basis of their past and feeling trapped in a cycle that they could not escape. These participants reported that police were constantly trying to 'pin something on them', as they faced the prospect of being 'in the system forever'.

One young man argued that police should instead recognise the disadvantage faced by his community to understand 'why young people behave the way they do', adding that 'they don't recognise the grief in my life'. Automated processes can be conceptualised as transforming individuals into 'pure information', divorced from the context and complexity of actual human lives (Haggerty & Ericson, 2000). In this regard, data-driven systems have the potential to amplify this pre-existing effect of distancing police intervention from its social context.

Young people who had come into conflict with the law sometimes shared their impressions of how police monitored them. One young South Sudanese Austra-lian painted a colourful picture of how local police identified their targets each day: 'Staff meeting in the morning, they're saying, "Apex, Apex, Apex. Going to fuck up all the kids." And then they think every nigga is Apex, bro. Apex doesn't even do crime'. These young people echoed the claims made by some youth workers that intensive policing was undermining the efforts of young people to change. One said: 'We're not crims no more, we don't want to be crims ... We're

---

[10]https://www.police.vic.gov.au/pso.

just trying to have fun'. However, they felt that the younger police in particular did not give them a chance: 'They treat you like an everyday criminal, you know what I mean, like an adult'. Another said, 'They don't even know what they're arresting kids for nowadays'. These accounts created an impression of a conveyor belt of surveillance and arrest, such that: 'They try so hard so you can't break out of the cycle even though you try'.

Although Australian police often attribute negative views about police to bad experiences in countries of origin, a South Sudanese Australian mother and grassroots community worker who participated in this research saw it differently. She was critical of the police tactics of relentless surveillance of past offenders, which she said were widely experienced within her community. She noted that in Africa 'people don't get police records'. Instead, the justice system just 'solves the problem' then 'leaves people be'; whereas in this country, she observed, 'a criminal record goes on forever'.

At the other end of the risk spectrum, young South Sudanese Australians in our study who had not broken any law still reported being stopped and asked, 'What's your name?' 'Where have you been?' 'How old are you?' 'Where are you going?' in an apparent effort by the police to map identities and friendship networks. Intelligence-led systems create a demand for data, and this has largely transformed police encounters with young people into exercises in the routine gathering of community intelligence. As a local police officer explained:

> Without information, there would be no way of predicting which youth are at the greatest risk of entering the criminal justice system ... sometimes that needs some form of intrusive discussions with them, in relation to gathering information.

Community workers sometimes identified this connection between routine street stops and data gathering. One experienced youth worker noted: 'The police don't give a reason why they are accusing them. It's so that the police can check and put it in their system'.

A focus group comprising young men of South Sudanese origin yielded numerous reports of unexplained stops. One young person said: 'We do get stopped a lot and questioned by police. "Where have you been?" "How old are you?" "Where are you going?"' Another said: 'We get stopped a lot at train stations. After basketball we take trains, we get stopped and questioned by police'. Another young man explained: 'They want to know who you are, where you live, know you are not a troublemaker'. This type of intrusive questioning was not confined to young people. A South Sudanese Australian woman said she was frequently followed by police cars when driving her friends home from church and questioned about where she lived. She had confronted them, saying: 'What do you think, when I didn't do anything wrong?'

Targeted surveillance is a technique widely applied to those defined as crimmigrant others (Franko, 2020). Information-gathering stops may also have a net-widening effect. Repeated contacts intended either to identify young people in need of early intervention or to map networks of connections between young people and other community members leave enduring traces within police systems. These records will mark a young person as having frequent contact with police, even in the absence of involvement in criminality, and will potentially fuel further such contacts, each with the potential to result in literal criminalisation. The South Sudanese Australian mothers interviewed for our study, without exception, expressed deep-seated fears that their children would find themselves in trouble with the law as a result of these unwanted encounters, through being either provoked or falsely accused of wrongdoing.

Gangs, Groups and Risky Places

While, on the one hand, senior police sought to communicate to the public that their media-induced fears about African gangs were overblown, at the local level any unofficial gathering of young people in public places might still be perceived and responded to as a public order threat. Windle (2008, p. 560) has reported that a multicultural liaison officer working with Dandenong police at the time of the racist murder of Liep Gony admitted that 'police often mistake groups of people who appear Sudanese for gangs'.[11] Disrupting gatherings of young people was considered a pre-emptive risk reduction tactic and one that offered further opportunities for data gathering. A local officer in our research explained:

> So part of our tasking will be, if we see groups of three, four, five males around, let's stop them, talk to them, find out what they are doing, get their details and hopefully deter them from any crime that they might be going to commit.

The use of such pre-emptive tactics by police is a hallmark of the securitisation of public places in which otherwise lawful activities are disrupted to prevent an anticipated threat (McCulloch & Wilson, 2016). Move-on experiences were widely reported by the young South Sudanese Australians in our study. One young man who was 'known to the police' provided the following example, which occurred in an outer suburb in the far south-east of Melbourne.

> Young person: We would just be kicking it after school or after work in the train station where the park is, you know, just where everyone hangs out, and police would rock up and [say], 'Okay, you, you, you, handcuffs now, get in the back'.

> Researcher: And, what do you think they would do after that? Take them to a police station?

---

[11]These specialist officers are operational police, not cultural diversity professionals.

Young person: Take them to the police station, have an interview or whatever.

Researcher: Because they were suspected of doing something?

Young person: Yeah.

Researcher: And, in your experience, were their suspicions right?

Young person: No.

Gathering in groups was widely seen by both the younger and older participants as a cultural practice that would not be perceived as a threat in their place of origin. In the exchange set out below between South Sudanese Australian mothers, misinterpretations about the threat posed by groups of young people in their local area were understood to be driven by the pervasive preoccupation with African gangs that reportedly extended into the education system.

Participant 1: It's not our kids. We don't know about gangs.

Participant 2: We don't know gangs. In our country we were in groups.

Participant 1: Not because they're gangs. Now [police] say that they are not allowed to walk in three.

Participant 3: That's right. Yeah ... that's the rule.

Participant 2: Yeah. Because as from three upwards you are considered as a gang. From three upwards you get together you are a gang group.

Participant 1: Even at school, they say that.

Participant 3: Yeah, even around school they are not allowed to be in one group like Sudanese.

These circumstances were seen to be directly related to the criminalisation of young people in their community:

Because now all the kids, they are in jail because they are walking like a group, when they going somewhere. If someone did something bad, all of them ... [All of them get in trouble?] Yes.[12]

Young South Sudanese Australians who participated in our study were aware of being perceived as dangerous by the police, and sometimes by the

---

[12]This may relate to anti-association laws introduced in Victoria to prevent young people from forming gangs (Enrique-Gomes, 2018).

wider community, especially when walking in a group. One young woman explained:

> There are not a lot of girls that play basketball like me, so I go home with boys in a group. And so, as a group we get seen as a threat.

As described in the following comment, the seemingly unwarranted fears of community members at times precipitated grossly disproportionate police intervention.

> It was around 11 and there were a few of us just mucking around after a basketball game. One of my friends fake-passed the ball to me and people around me got upset and called the police on us. There were six cars that came and saw us in basketball gear in the mall. The police surrounded us, and pinned us to the floor. It was excessive and disproportionate. This happened multiple times. We were 13–14 years old.

In another example, a young community leader recounted an experience in which he came across a small group of South Sudanese Australians – all early teenagers – who were being aggressively targeted by police while merely 'hanging out with other kids'.

> The kids were just having a laugh, on school holidays. I got my phone out and tried to record things because the police were so aggressive towards them and I wasn't happy. I told myself to stand back, but I saw the whole thing and I couldn't stand back for my community. This went on for 30 minutes, and I went on and asked the kids, 'What have you done wrong?' They hadn't done anything wrong. The police were accusing them of doing things they haven't done. The police have the power because they have a uniform. They are asking them, 'Why are you hanging out with other kids?'

Overall, the disruption by police of groups of young South Sudanese Australians seemed to be justified either on the basis of some unspecified threat posed by these gatherings or of the perceived risk of possible future harm these groups posed to the wider community. In turn, some young people said that they found the police practice of arriving in large numbers in these situations to be extremely threatening: 'They come in a group with a lot of weapons. They always have their hand on their gun'. The heightened police responses recounted in this section indicate that the gathering in public of young South Sudanese Australians had perhaps become too readily aligned with Police Commissioner Ashton's characterisation of 'street gang behaviour'.

The Production of Racialised Policing

Individual Racism

The risk-based system that underpins the policing of young people in Melbourne's south-east has clearly generated high levels of surveillance and intervention for the South Sudanese Australians who took part in our study. This brings us to the question of how race plays out in these systems and in the one-on-one police encounters reported by our research participants.

In relation to individual racism, serious examples of racial vilification and racially motivated police violence were reported by some young people. Just as they sometimes identified police who were particularly supportive and under-standing, participants also identified individual officers who were especially prone to hostile and racist behaviour. One young man who had been in conflict with the law named a particular detective who would 'chase' him around, hurling racist abuse and threatening to 'make your life a living hell'. Another described being handcuffed, punched and then told, 'I'd hate to be your fucking colour, I'd hate to fucking be black'. And a youth worker reported that the young South Sudanese Australians she supported were often called 'black cunts' by certain local police.

Racist abuse could easily arise when young people challenged their discriminatory treatment.

> Yeah, one time at [the train station] they go, 'No you can't come in'. I go, 'What the fuck? Because I'm the only black guy?'. I go, 'So only me, out of all these people? Oh good, racist cunt'. And he goes, 'You know what bro? I am racist'.

It was widely conceded that 'some cops are more discriminatory than others, some are more fair'. But young people sometimes felt that racialised targeting was expressly built into policing practice:

> As soon as you get arrested, you've got to think about what they say in the staff meeting. "These black kids, blah-blah-blah" ... At the end of the day, they're still going to do that shit to us, [whether we are] doing wrong or not.

Another young person believed that targeting African youths was expressly rewarded within the police organisation:

> That's the easy way to get up high in their career. I've been here more than 10 years. I've seen recruits who are now sergeants from their work in the African community ... They get privileges. That's how they end up treating us.

Some young people reported physical violence. One focus group participant recounted being seriously assaulted by local police.

> I was bashed once by the police at a party. There was a fight
> happening after the party. I was trying to stop the fight. The police
> was spraying everyone with pepper spray … They took me
> somewhere and beat me. I didn't even do anything. I had to run.
> They would have left me there and bashed me. They opened my lip
> and I had to go to the hospital for two days.

Participants sometimes expressed the view that police violence was particularly directed towards their community. One young person said that singling out black people for violent treatment was 'like a power trip' for some police officers, which he likened to a form of warfare.

> Researcher: And there were how many police officers at that
> point?
>
> Interviewee: I can't even, can't even count … there's like five, six
> on me and there's about five, six, seven, maybe more. But there's
> undercover cops, there's the sergeant, there's PSOs, there, all of
> them. They've all come fucking to go to war.

Systemic Racism

Beyond these examples of individual racism, racialised understandings of 'how policing is done' can become embedded in routine practices, without either direct instructions or deliberate rewards for targeting certain groups. The concept of systemic racism is still poorly understood by Victorian police members, who often speak as if 'racial profiling' only occurs when race is written explicitly into operating procedures. Police in Dandenong were adamant that race was not a factor used directly in any of their predictive models. However, in the absence of explanations for why they were being stopped, young people sometimes attributed their experiences to systemic racism which, in effect, attached the label of 'crimmigrant other' to their entire community. Police were said to stereotype people, and one young man said, 'I don't know why police are stopping me, just for being a black person'. Someone else commented, 'It's more like you're conscious of what colour and nationality I am. If I am seen by the cops, I know I'll be looked at in a certain way'. An experienced community worker described how suspicion about actual crime could be dispersed across non-offending sections of the community:

> Because they are vulnerable, police can intimidate them … "The
> person who committed these offences is African, so you being
> African fit the description of the criminal, so it must be you."

A common experience was that police would pull someone over, assume that they were unlicensed or driving under the influence of drugs or alcohol and then ask 'serious questions' that 'make you feel targeted'. One young person observed,

> It happens all the time, I get stopped for no reason. Police just come and hope they can find something wrong with your car, driving without a licence, etcetera. They find nothing and they just walk away and feel ashamed, but they don't say why they stopped you.

A young South Sudanese Australian reported that her partner had been stopped by a large group of police and falsely accused of stealing a car and carrying drugs: 'It came out of nowhere; he's not known to police. I think they picked on him because of his skin colour'.

Although this study produced no statistics to 'prove' that young South Sudanese Australians are being stopped at a disproportionate rate in the south-eastern suburbs of Melbourne, there were numerous first-hand reports of these young people being specifically targeted on the basis of race. This form of targeting of people with an African appearance was considered to be explicit and routine, and not necessarily animated by individual racism. One young person explained:

> They are doing their jobs; we understand that. But we get picked due to the colour of our skins. They look bored. They don't care about the white or Asian who is doing the same thing. They come straight to the black person.

Another young man described being approached by police and questioned while his white companion was ignored: 'I felt really sad. Was it racist? I just kept it in'.

Several young men who took part in a group interview said that they were routinely 'racially profiled', giving examples of being singled out from mixed groups in shopping centres, at train stations and on the street:

> Let's just say you see 12 white kids walking around at 12 a.m. and you see a group of Sudanese kids walking around at night. Like, it's more than likely that the Sudanese kids are going to get pulled over instead of the white kids, you know what I mean? And, like, I just think that is bullshit because, like, how is that fair?

These accounts of police selectively targeting young people of African heritage were often reinforced by the accounts of youths from other backgrounds. One young Pasifika participant recalled hearing a police officer say:

"You know how those Sudanese people are". And I was just like, "Woah, well how are they?" They are always going to have an outlook on a certain race as being criminals.

Another young Pasifika person recounted the following experience at a party.

I was with a guy who was big and black, and there were a lot of people there, and out of all the people [the police] stopped and pulled over to talk to, it was the black guy who was the only sober one of the group. They harassed him and threatened to take him to the station when there were other fights going on around him.

Although many Pasifika youths also reported being treated as if they were a threat to others, it was widely believed that an informal hierarchy of racialised policing was in operation, with young South Sudanese Australians at the 'top'. One young South Sudanese participant claimed:

There is a lot of discrimination. There used to be fights between Africans and New Zealanders at Dandenong train station. When the African gets beaten up they don't do anything. When it is the other way round they follow up.

A young Pasifika person noted:

Like, don't get me wrong, I'm not being racist or anything, but the Sudanese, you know, they're always targeting them ... I mean, there's other people out there, they are doing a lot worse shit than what they are, and I don't like that. It's always a specific targeted race.

An experienced Pasifika youth worker noted that her own community had 'been there first' as prime targets for police but had now been supplanted in the hierarchy of 'crimmigrant others' by South Sudanese Australians. She attributed this to the media-generated crisis around African youths and the resulting stigma that had been 'only created a few years ago' the implications of which she regularly observed playing out on the streets: The Australian kids get walked past. [The police] go straight to the Sudanese, and then they just move them on and start harassing them ....

This youth worker then gave a particular example:

And then they went to our [Pasifika] kids. I said, 'No, leave them alone ... You can have the white ones'. But they didn't go near them. They just walked around them and carried on.

'Hardwiring' Racism

So how might the risk-based systems discussed earlier be contributing to the race-based targeting described by South Sudanese Australians in this part of Melbourne? Racialised targeting considerably predates the advent of predictive technologies and is often embedded in cultural understandings of how police work is done (Bowling & Phillips, 2007; Cunneen, 2006). But evidence is mounting that data-driven systems can both 'hardwire' and amplify pre-existing practices that disproportionately target certain groups (Williams & Kind, 2019). Critics have cautioned that, while presented as entirely factual and neutral, '[a]lgorithms, like people, can be subject to bias, either built in – wittingly or otherwise, by those who program them – or learnt by the machines themselves' (Seccombe, 2019). The building-in of systemic discrimination based on race or ethnic identity stems from existing patterns of differential policing reflected in the source data, which is then 'hardwired' into the system and guides future practice. A review of predictive systems used by police across Europe concluded that:

> The belief in the independence and objectivity of data-driven policing solutions and in particular, predictive policing programmes will send law enforcement officers to monitor and detect crimes in the same already over-policed communities.
> (Williams & Kind, 2019, p. 15)

These systems also have the propensity to 'launder' the effect of race by disguising it in purportedly objective measures of risk (Goddard & Myers, 2017). The propensity of automated systems to consistently over-predict the risk associated with racialised groups has been described as the 'digital racialization of risk' (Ugwudike, 2020, p. 484). Ugwudike argues that the 'logic of validation' encourages the 'belief that excluding social categories such as race and using complex numerical analysis eliminates bias [and] ensures scientific objectivity' (p. 483). Even more damagingly perhaps, this can mask the need to take into account persistent discrimination across social institutions. In the United Kingdom, for example, an astonishing 78% of entries on the London Metropolitan Police 'Gangs Matrix' were classified as black, reflecting the fact that 'racial bias in the database' had become 'institutionalised in police practice' (Bridges, n.d.). Closer to home, the research on the Suspect Targeting Management Plan in New South Wales mentioned earlier concluded that the system disproportionately targeted young people from Aboriginal and Torres Strait Islander backgrounds, who made up 44% of all recorded 'targets', while constituting less than 3% of the state population (Sentas & Pandolfini, 2017).

Victoria Police has not made public any statistical information about its risk-based systems that would enable a systematic analysis of any discriminatory outcomes associated with their use. However, our research did indicate that a desire to collect information from non-offending young people could be driving intelligence-gathering stops targeted disproportionately at South Sudanese Australians. The police interviewed in our study noted that, as South Sudanese

Australians constitute an 'emerging community',[13] there were significant gaps in the government data used to identify 'at-risk' youths for early intervention. This was said to create a greater reliance on information collected directly from young people through street stops. A local officer explained:

> The system is really good for the WASP kind of background of youth. It's not for the new and emerging youth within the community, because there's an under-reporting of family violence, under-reporting of missing youth, so we're looking to see how often those youth are being checked on the street with YNOs.

It could reasonably be concluded, therefore, that the demand for data to drive predictive tools aimed at identifying candidates for early intervention contributes to some degree to disproportionate police intervention in relation to young South Sudanese Australians.

A corollary of targeted intelligence-gathering practices is that increased police-initiated contacts may themselves feed into automated systems in ways that unreasonably inflate calculations of risk, as explained by Ugwudike (2020, p. 493):

> A racializing effect of this is that if Machine Learning varieties of risk prediction technologies are trained on the datasets, they could, for example, learn to identify indices of criminal justice processing such as arrests or having 'been stopped by the police' (Kehl et al., 2017: 24) as predictors of recidivism. This could disadvantage racialized people, particularly black people, given their disproportionate vulnerability to unwarranted police intervention.
>
> (Phillips & Bowling, 2017)

We were told in our research that PSOs in the Dandenong area in particular are encouraged to interact with, and get to know, young people from diverse communities as part of their community engagement efforts. In this regard, one young South Sudanese Australian man described how he had been approached by police on his way home while walking with a 'white friend'. The officers questioned him, but not his friend. When he asked if he had done something wrong, they said, 'No, we are just trying to know you'.

Even when these encounters are relatively courteous, repeated stops by police in the absence of offending marks the targets of these stops as crimmigrants who are subjected to higher levels of routine surveillance than other sections of the community and expected to justify their presence in public places. While intelligence-gathering stops may be perceived by police and PSOs as simply a routine aspect of

---

[13]This is the term used within Victoria Police to denote recently arrived or marginalised migrant communities.

operational policing, our study revealed that the young people subjected to these stops experience a wide range of emotions as a result, including feeling 'humiliated', 'powerless', 'judged', 'traumatised', 'disrespected', 'misunderstood', 'stigmatised', 'not trustworthy', like a 'bit of a threat' and many other reactions that may challenge their sense of identity and belonging (Weber, 2020b). In the remainder of this chapter we consider how unwarranted police encounters help to construct South Sudanese Australians as, at best, not belonging and, at worst, as 'symbolic assailants' who threaten the security of the wider community, while ultimately undermining their own sense of collective security.

Policing and Belonging

The Politics of Belonging

Because 'belonging' is a relational concept, and thereby subject to (unequal) relations of power, Yuval-Davis (2011) has argued that a 'politics of belonging' arises whenever boundaries of inclusion and exclusion are enacted or contested. This is important because majority attitudes based on 'tacit understandings of who belongs and who does not' are often considered more important than formal policies in cultivating a sense of 'having a place in a community' (Simonsen, 2016, p. 1153). Police can be crucial actors in the politics of belonging because of their perceived status as government representatives. Procedural justice theorist Tom Tyler (1997) asserts that, during encounters with members of the public, police communicate whether or not individuals are respected members of communities. In practice, police conceptions of who belongs and is to be respected may be highly racialised, so that police interventions produce and deepen racially constructed divides (Parmar, 2017).

To explore the role of police in the politics of belonging, we need to consider how the targeted police actions described in earlier sections of this chapter might be perceived by various audiences within the wider community. A youth worker interviewed in our study was clearly aware of the wider implications of police intervention in terms of reinforcing public perceptions of the dangerousness of particular racially defined groups of young people.

> When you're having police talk to young people and there are people that are there in that space who are witnessing all of this, that impacts on the way they perceive that. And if that person's innocent, hasn't really committed – done anything, and they are being picked on by police officers, then you can imagine what type of conclusions people are drawing as to what type of person that young person is ... I mean, I see them, people in the public spaces when they see groups of certain kinds of young people standing together, they'll cross the road.

Another community worker accused local police of 'fearmongering' by telling 'white people' not to park their cars in certain areas, apparently in order to avoid victimisation by African youths. A young South Sudanese Australian explained that 'when other people see black kids being stopped by police, then it gives them an idea that black people are not good, that they are bad'. And a South Sudanese mother told us that unwarranted visits to her house by groups of police had prompted her neighbours to complain to the housing provider that her home was a 'gangster house'.

Some research participants attributed discriminatory police actions to the influence of wider dynamics within the politics of belonging. In particular, they saw the discriminatory treatment of their communities at the hands of police as being strongly shaped by community fears and attitudes. One young South Sudanese Australian summed it up simply: 'Police make you feel like you don't belong because they are influenced by society'. This influence was informed by the expectations of shopkeepers, teachers, public transport staff and passengers and anyone from the wider community who felt they could readily call on police to intervene in their favour. This perception – that police are there to serve Anglo-Australian residents at the expense of outsider groups – was expressed succinctly by one South Sudanese Australian woman in our study, who said: 'Police are good for some people, but not for us'.

One young man recalled an altercation in which he was the aggrieved party, but said that 'the police made me feel like I wasn't a victim, but like I was doing something wrong'. A South Sudanese Australian mother lamented that police 'don't listen to black people, only white people'. She recounted the story of when she had slightly touched another vehicle in a car park. After checking that there was no damage to either car she had driven off, only to be chased by the male driver who had yelled at her and called the police. When the police arrived, she claimed that they were not interested in looking at the lack of damage or in listening to her, but instead issued her with an on-the-spot fine. On the other hand, she noted that the police had done nothing about the racist abuse directed towards her by the occupants of the other vehicle, which had traumatised her children.

The focus group participants gave examples in which community members appeared to view them with fear and suspicion. Some young people claimed that individuals would hold onto their handbags or cross the road when they saw them approaching. Others said, 'You feel like they are going to look at you like you did something wrong'; 'People are scared to sit next to us on the train'; and 'If you walk up to people, they walk the other way. They put their phones in their pockets. No one thinks that you are innocent'. Someone else observed,

> People from my community feel like they don't belong. It relates to Apex. People at shopping centres assume that black young people will take stuff from them and don't feel safe.

One young man said that these kinds of experiences made him worry that some sections of the community might 'take things into their own hands' because they think that a 'group of black youths are a threat'.

Policing, Community and Media

The role of the media was sometimes mentioned by participants as driving community perceptions, which then translated into harsh and discriminatory policing. One young person said,

> I feel like those feelings don't come from the cops, it's more from society, from the news and social media, pointing out Africans and Sudanese etcetera. It makes you feel like you don't belong.

An adult community member lamented: 'We are not getting acceptance in the community. You have to be something special to get acceptance'. Another young South Sudanese Australian noted that different waves of immigrants had been subjected to negative media representations over the years. He questioned the impression being created that the most recent arrivals posed a unique threat to Australian society, saying, 'As if this is new. They're acting like this is new, bro'.

One young person had noticed a shift in police practice away from trust-building activities towards more hostile interventions, which he attributed explicitly to inflammatory media reporting:

> Before the whole African attention in the media, police used to come to the school as part of a reaching out program. We went with them on foot patrol. We played soccer and basketball against them. It was around 2007–8 before everything was in the media.

Even a group of young people who had experienced severe racial vilification and racially motived violence at the hands of police considered the media to be largely to blame.

> Youth worker: So, do you think a lot of them are racist or do you think they've been affected by all the media stuff?
>
> Young person 1: Media. The media has a lot to do with it.
>
> Young person 2: They're not racist, I know they're not racist.
>
> Young person 1: The media hypes up the situation a lot more than –
>
> Youth worker: They're calling you black cunts though.
>
> Young person 1: Because they make it sound like the cops aren't doing their job, and then the cops react to that and then they go harder.

While the participants in this study tended to portray the media as exercising an independent effect on police, this overlooks the role that police members play as 'primary definers' (Hall et al., 1978) in media reporting that associates young African Australians with criminality. In a 2008 analysis of media representations,

Windle (2008, p. 563) concluded that '[r]acialisation of African refugees in the Australian media appears to find its proximate source in the activation of race as an explanatory category amongst police'. While senior police, at times, may have intervened to mitigate racialised discourses about African gangs, Windle found that the media systematically, and mostly uncritically, relied on 'local officers' of varying ranks to define problems of youth crime in their area, allowing dominant police framings about 'riots', 'gangs', 'hotspots', 'packs', unverified crime statistics and the supposed 'culture of violence' imported into Australia by South Sudanese Australians to remain unchallenged.

While the police role in shaping media discourse was not mentioned by the participants in our research, curbing the influence of the media was seen to be an essential condition for changing police practice. One youth worker who believed the media 'needs to be held responsible for what they report' reserved particular criticism for a television documentary that had unfairly singled out African youths:

> If you watch those videos, it was just the Sudanese kids. It wasn't funny, because our kids were there, the Australian kids were there, everyone was there, but they only put on the television the Sudanese kids ... If you dealt with the media as much as you're going to deal with the police, you'll take away half of that fire. Because that's where it all starts, is the media reporting.

The potential role played by police as 'primary definers' in producing that narrative about a racialised and seemingly homogeneous group of 'crimmigrant others' evidently remains largely invisible, concealed within the machinery of news reporting.

The Differential Distribution of Security

'Now We Don't Have Any Security'

In the previous section, we explored how the racialised narrative of a law and order crisis depicting African youths as a threat to suburban communities impacted local policing in south-eastern Melbourne. Our research also revealed many instances in which negative experiences with police had in turn generated feelings of substantial distrust and insecurity among South Sudanese Australians. Policing scholar Ian Loader has observed that, as an institution, police deliver 'a small but vital component of the resources of secure belonging' (2006, p. 210). The pairing of these two concepts – 'security' and 'belonging' – acknowledges the connection between feelings of acceptance and belonging and a sense of having a secure and stable place in the world. Indeed, feelings of safety, both physical and emotional, were strongly identified with a sense of belonging by the young people in our study. Some young people reported feeling 'worried', 'paranoid', 'anxious', 'scared', 'stressed', 'unsafe' or 'frightened' as a result of their interactions with police.

A previous study by Victoria University researchers in another part of Melbourne found that police were seen by young people, particularly those from Pasifika and South Sudanese Australian backgrounds, to

> ...simultaneously enhance the safety of young people by their *presence* in the local area – but also place the safety of young people at risk by their *behaviour* in the local area.
>
> (Grossman & Sharples, 2010, p. xiv, italics in original)

Moreover, Run (2013, p. 22) has observed that unnecessary and intrusive encounters with police create a 'double burden' for South Sudanese Australians, reawakening the 'well-founded fear of being targeted on the basis of race that these refugees fled in the first place'.

The young people in our study reported that they dealt with unwanted police encounters by resisting police intervention, by trying to defuse potential conflict or, more commonly, by trying to avoid any contact at all. But avoidance strategies themselves could become a source of protracted anxiety. One youth worker lamented that young people were being taught to 'tiptoe around everywhere so they're not going to get into trouble', adding that 'our kids should be able to go do what they want'. The advice of one young South Sudanese Australian man to his younger siblings was to avoid trouble by simply staying home: 'I tell my little brother, "You better be at home", simple'. In this vein, researchers who studied the impact of a risk-based policing system used in New South Wales on Indigenous Australians reported that many young people targeted by that system 'felt they couldn't leave the home', significantly disrupting their ability to have a normal life (Sentas, 2017; Sentas & Pandolfini, 2017).

South Sudanese Australian mothers who took part in our study all had stories to tell about incidents involving their children, themselves or someone they knew that left them feeling anxious and insecure. During the interviews they exuded a palpable fear about the constant threat of criminalisation of their children through unwarranted police action. When their children were outside the home, these mothers were perpetually worried, waiting for a knock on the door. One woman recounted how she had discouraged her son from even walking on the street at night, after a frightening experience with police:

> I say, "Oh, it's what I told you last time. Don't go outside at night. Don't go to the gym. Avoid everything." He said, "No. I can go." I said, "OK … Now try to pray for yourself because, if something happened tomorrow, I can't help you."

Another South Sudanese Australian mother recounted how her 13-year-old daughter had been stopped by police at a train station for no reason, while white girls had been let through. She was now afraid to let her children go out on their own or to attend parties with 'all black people' because police 'might do something'. Another woman said that it was 'scary' for her children to go to the shops because of discriminatory treatment by security guards. Young South Sudanese people were said to be afraid to give their correct name and address when questioned because police 'could come back later and say you did things'. Mothers also expressed their fears that police might plant evidence on their children, for example, by 'putting something in their bag when they search it'. One mother claimed that police used their recording devices selectively after provoking young people in order to incriminate them: 'They stop the recording and then they try to push our kids ... This is what I want to say'.

Police actions could also create unsafe situations for young South Sudanese Australians in more indirect ways. One woman recalled how police officers, possibly PSOs, had arbitrarily prevented her children from returning home on the train late at night, putting them in danger.

> I had a call from my son. We just – he was with his old brothers and his sisters. It was around 10 to 11, so they call me and say, 'Mum, can you please come and pick us up from the train station?' And I said, 'Why do I pick you up from the station, like, in Dandenong? I told you guys to train and then I will come, and we will meet in [another] station'. And they said, 'The police don't like us to go there'. And I said, 'Why?' They said, 'We don't know'.

A youth worker recounted a similar story. A young South Sudanese Australian man had attended an event run by her organisation in a park adjoining Dandenong train station and had returned upset after being refused permission to enter the station when attempting to return home.

Somewhat ironically, since 'home invasion' is one category of crime that has been discursively linked with African Australians in some media reporting, other personal security concerns arose from the intrusive and disrespectful way that police were said to enter the homes of African Australians. One youth worker explained: 'They, like, burst into little kids' rooms ... I understand they have to search the whole house but they're really rude to parents'. A South Sudanese Australian mother described how police entered houses in a 'shock way' and reported a specific incident that had caused her young children to become 'really scared'.

> This happened once in – I guess it was two months. I have 10 years old and a six years old girl. So, the police come into my house, which they was looking for a white boy ... So, my kids, even my son who was, like, really crying and he couldn't understand what's going on. And he asked me, like, 'Mum, is that the way the police always do?'

Another woman whose house had been entered aggressively by police explained how this had affected her feeling of security and her trust in police as providers of security for her family.

> What I know is if maybe someone try to come and enter your house to do whatever, or you're not feeling safe, you have to call

> the police. If you call the police and they will come in this way, do
> you feel safe? Do we feel safe? ... So, we need them to treat the
> people in a good way. We need to feel safe, because it's their job to
> look after us and protect us.

The irony that the police, whose role is to promote community safety and
protection, were often a source of insecurity for this section of the community was
not lost on the participants in our study. One young South Sudanese Australian
explained: 'For me it's not police, but the laws that help to protect you. The police
itself do not always protect you'. A South Sudanese Australian woman provided a
more expansive explanation of the role of local police in the production of
insecurity through both the under- and over-policing of her community.

> So, police should be the one to be there for you. And then imagine
> if the police themselves are your worry. They are your fear ... This
> is the problem with our young ones. So the police is a source of
> fear for them. So they are always in ... defensive position because
> they know the police is there, not for me. Not because they are
> criminals, not because they are doing something wrong. No. It's
> just because the police doesn't like me.

Another South Sudanese Australian mother summed up the wider implications
of the treatment of her community by police and others as follows:

> We brought those kids in this country to have a good future. Now
> we feel sorry because we didn't get what we want ... We came here
> because we know this country is secure. Now we don't have any
> security.

Securing Citizenship

In insecure times, citizenship – whether conceived as a form of legal protection
and guarantee of rights or as an informal social construct denoting respect and
social acceptance – offers a crucial source of secure belonging. Security scholar
Lucia Zedner (2006, p. 427) has observed that populations are increasingly
divided into those who are included or excluded from the 'orbit of protection', due
to securitisation agendas that typically produce a form of security for the majority
at the expense of marginalised groups (see also Zedner, 2010). Citizenship, both
legally and socially defined, is central to being included in this 'orbit of protection'. Once again, police can be seen to play a defining role in this dynamic.

> [P]olice patrol the boundaries of citizenship: the citizenship of
> those who are 'respectable' is secured, while those who attack
> the state exclude themselves from citizenship. Between these

extremes are those whose claim to citizenship is insecure and needs repeatedly to be negotiated. Police are the de facto arbiters of their citizenship.

(Waddington, 1999, p. 41)

The interactions with police cited by South Sudanese Australians in this chapter in which they were not accorded the same level of respect or protection as other community members were sometimes interpreted in these terms. As one young person put it:

If the police do listen to you then that means they value you as a human or as a citizen, and when they don't it's like they're telling you "You're not one of us."

Closely associated with citizenship is the question of rights. One South Sudanese Australian woman perceived her community's relationship with the police in terms of both citizenship and rights: 'So nobody has rights. They don't have rights in the street. What if [the police] don't do it right?' Her expectation was for members of her community to be recognised and supported as equal and full citizens:

When we come here we think we belong here. We are citizens here, not just come and go back. But not any more because of the crisis created by media and government.

For South Sudanese Australians who lack the protections of legal citizenship, an additional source of insecurity is the prospect of deportation following a criminal conviction. Crimmigrant others are marked not just for surveillance and the exercise of penal power but also for physical exclusion. As Franko (2020, p. 167) notes: 'The crimmigrant other comes up against the desire to punish those who are different, and the determination to exclude those who do not belong'.

High levels of contact with the police, whether or not such contact results in convictions for serious offences, can trigger visa cancellation under Section 501 of the *Migration Act*, even of permanent visas (Billings, 2019; Weber & Powell, 2020). Visa cancellation then renders a non-citizen liable to mandatory detention and deportation. This is a process in which police play a key role. As the de facto arbiters of citizenship for those with insecure legal or social status, police can be understood as the gatekeepers to the particular applications of penal power used to exclude crimmigrant others. As Franko (2020, p. 10) explains:

A defining feature of the crimmigrant other is, therefore, that he or she is not a member, or that his/her claim to membership is tenuous and can be revoked through the use of penal power. This type of penality, which is geared towards banishment and exclusion from the nation, represents a significant break from the ways in which penal power was used in the past.

At the time of writing, Melbourne-based members of the Visa Cancellation Working Group, which includes lawyers representing non-citizens facing deportation on these grounds, have reported that they are encountering increasing numbers of young South Sudanese Australians among their caseloads.[14] Many of these cases arise after individuals are referred to immigration authorities by police – often identified, erroneously according to the legal representatives, as gang members. This is suggestive of a direct, although behind the scenes, role for police in following through the law and order crisis over 'African gangs' to its logical conclusion.

Ultimately, decisions over visa cancellation are made by immigration officials, not police. The real possibility of deportation as a result of being labelled a gang member is apparent from the instructions used by immigration officials to cancel visas under Section 501 of the Migration Act. The Character Case Allocation Matrix lists 'violent youth gangs' in the highest risk category, alongside organised child exploitation, murder, crimes against humanity and matters of national security, all of which are to be dealt with personally by the Home Affairs Minister.[15] Indeed, violent youths are apparently considered a greater threat to the Australian community than serious crimes of violence against women and children and all other forms of violent offending, all of which can be dealt with by departmental delegates. The heightened perception of threat associated with the 'youth gang' label, and the fact that this criterion is the only one within the Matrix based on an attributed status rather than conviction for a recognised criminal act, suggests that deportation following designation by police as a gang member could be the ultimate endgame in the law and order crisis over 'African gangs'.

At the time of writing, South Sudanese Australians – some of whom have the protection of legal citizenship – do not feature prominently within official statistics on forced and voluntary removals from Australia.[16,17] One report suggests that between 50 and 100 citizens of South Sudan have had their visas cancelled under s501 since 2014, with fewer than 10 actually removed (Fernandes, 2020). Even so, the threat of deportation has emerged as a source of extreme insecurity within communities. One South Sudanese mother noted: 'They can take your citizenship. They can strip it. They have power'.[18] While the federal Department of Home Affairs is responsible for immigration enforcement, our research found that local police were often perceived by community members to be the initiators

---

[14]Personal communication, Visa Cancellation Working Group.

[15]Freedom of Information reference number FA 191201189 available from FOA Disclosure Logs https://www.homeaffairs.gov.au/access-and-accountability/freedom-of-information/disclosure-logs/2020.

[16]There are no reliable statistics available on rates of Australian citizenship within this group and variability in the legal citizenship of those who may identify as South Sudanese Australians further complicates the picture.

[17]Source: FOI request FA 19/11/01582 provided by Department of Home Affairs to Dr Brandy Cochrane on 21 May 2020.

[18]Note that s501 deportation actually involves visa cancellation rather than citizenship stripping and applies only to non-citizens.

of deportation proceedings: 'They are starting to dispose of people ... They are deporting people from my community. They are being hard on crime and they are reporting the figures'. One participant explained the significant impact the threat of deportation was having on feelings of security within her community:

> Now in this country we are really worried ... Because our 'back home', we don't have a 'back home'. If our country is good enough, all of us, we can say we need to go back. It's not just the kids. Because now the government, they start something. They say, 'You need to send the kids back home'. Where do they send them?

Indeed, practical difficulties in effecting the deportation of South Sudanese Australians arising from ongoing conflict and instability and bureaucratic obstacles to obtaining the necessary documentation in the country of origin may in part explain the relative invisibility of this national group within official deportation statistics. At the time of writing, an undisclosed number of South Sudanese Australians are believed to be in prolonged immigration detention following visa cancellation, unable to be deported because of prohibitions against the refoulement of refugees to danger (Fernandes, 2020). While their legal categorisation as refugees provides protection from physical expulsion in the interests of their own security, it seems that their informal categorisation as crimmigrants mandates their indefinite detention to protect the security of the wider community.

Despite these concerted efforts to exclude them, young South Sudanese Australians were perceived by some members of the parental generation of their community as having a greater claim to belonging in Australia than to the country of their birth. As one woman explained: 'Our young people are white like you. I tell the community they are not ours any more. They are white. We cannot agree to send them back'. However, the idea that their children identified culturally as 'white' was clearly not reflected in their treatment by police or their acceptance by sections of the wider community – a subject that will be explored further in the final chapter.

Conclusion: Policing the 'African Crime' Crisis

We have argued in previous chapters that conservative politicians have been the main driver of the media-fuelled crisis over African gangs, assisted by a partisan and sensationalising media. However, police have also played a part, particularly at the local level, both in responding to and reinforcing this phenomenon.

Although at times Victoria Police representatives have attempted to restore balance in the distorted public debate about 'African crime', the picture that has emerged in this chapter about the police role at the local level is a mixed one. Testimonies from youth workers and community members in Melbourne's south-east revealed significant experiences of both racialised targeting and racist violence from frontline police, which some people attributed to the prevailing climate of hostile media reporting and resultant public fears. These reported experiences are consistent with the (informal) designation of South Sudanese Australians as 'crimmigrant others', rendering them liable to heightened surveillance, the application of penal power and exclusion (Franko, 2020).

While police clearly respond to community demands as they see them, our analysis illustrates how police have also reinforced public perceptions of South Sudanese Australians as 'crimmigrant others'. This has occurred both directly, through statements to the media, and indirectly, through their unwitting role in a 'politics of belonging', in which messages of danger and otherness are communicated to the public through visible police interventions and racialised targeting. In particular, the breaking up of groups of non-offending young people as a pre-emptive measure, ostensibly to prevent possible future offending, potentially reinforces the imagery of 'African gangs' to the wider community.

Despite avowed efforts by Victoria Police to eradicate so-called racial profiling, the findings from our research with young South Sudanese Australians living in the south-east of Melbourne reinforce the view that authoritative messages from senior management are unlikely to trickle down to practice at the coalface if external factors such as community expectations, or internal factors such as systemic practices and rank-and-file culture, are pulling in opposing directions (Chan, 1997). Our enquiries led to the conclusion that risk-based systems used to identify 'youth network offenders', while they reportedly do not incorporate explicit information about race, could nevertheless amplify systemic racism by 'hardwiring' in pre-existing discriminatory practices.

Young people identified through this system as 'high risk' due to their previous offences were likely to experience intensive police monitoring and enforcement action, rather than be provided with support, which could make it difficult to escape from a cycle of offending and reinforce their ongoing non-acceptance as community members. Systems for identifying 'at-risk' youth in order to direct them to support services and away from future offending, although seemingly well-intentioned, were found to create demand for 'community intelligence', which could, in turn, expose young South Sudanese Australians to intrusive street stops, potentially increasing the possibility of future criminalisation.

Hostile or intrusive actions by police, seemingly legitimated by exaggerated public concern over African gangs and crime, have contributed to distrust of police and a widespread sense of fear and non-belonging among the South Sudanese Australians who participated in our study. This betrayal is felt all the more keenly by a refugee community who came to Australia expressly in search of security. The fears conveyed by the South Sudanese Australian mothers who participated in this study included fear over the criminalisation of young people, their physical mistreatment by police and ultimately deportation to another location where they could face even greater danger.

As Franko (2020, p. 3) explains in relation to the construction of 'crimmigrant others':

> Immigrants are no longer people in need of protection, or a potential
> source of labour; they have been turned into rule-breakers and

criminal offenders .... Their presence is associated with illegality and crime.

Although this process of othering is multi-dimensional and depends on a range of wider environmental conditions, police in Melbourne bear a share of the responsibility for helping to construct and maintain this conflation in relation to African Australians.

Chapter 5

Impact on the South Sudanese and Wider Australian Communities

Within the Australian context, there is significant research documenting the challenges faced by incoming African settlers (Abur & Spaaij, 2016; Baak, 2019; Chivaura, 2019; Forrest & Dunn, 2013; Khan & Pedersen, 2010; Udah & Singh, 2019; Windle, 2008). While various support services can be accessed in the three to five years post arrival, it is clear that the challenges of settlement can continue long past the settlement period (Maher, 2018). The process of needing to adapt to new legal and social systems, navigate new cultures and access education and employment is common to many incoming immigrants, but there is an additional layer of complexity and difficulty for refugee immigrants that further compounds the upheaval of relocation. For new residents from a South Sudanese background, there have been accompanying experiences of racism, profiling and discrimination that intensify the challenges of the migration experience.

This chapter explores the impact of the post-Moomba criminalisation of the Sudanese and South Sudanese communities. Its approach is twofold. First, it focusses on the disruptive nature of media, police and political attention on individuals, families and communities as detailed in the previous chapters and the resulting harm done to Sudanese/South Sudanese Australians' post-settlement sense of identity and belonging. Second, it examines the altered perceptions about African people held by the wider Australian community, with a focus on stereotyping, fear of victimisation and general sentiments.

As detailed in Chapter 2, racism and discrimination targeting South Sudanese people as a result of political and media attention was not only the result of the aftermath of Moomba 2016, but actually began in 2007 with the comments of the former Minister of Immigration, Kevin Andrews. After the murder of Liep Gony, Andrews publicly stated that South Sudanese immigrants were unable to adjust to Australian society and had failed to integrate (Wright, 2007). While it was later revealed that Mr Gony was murdered by two white men, Andrews refused to apologise for his comments and the media reported the incident in such a way that young people from the South Sudanese community were depicted as the 'problem group' rather than a targeted population that had been victimised (Dawes et al., 2014; Windle, 2008).

Place, Race and Politics, 89–101

Published under exclusive licence by Emerald Publishing Limited
doi:10.1108/978-1-80043-045-720211005

The Moomba 'riots' of 2016 saw a turning point in the levels of prejudice and discrimination experienced by South Sudanese communities. Despite these communities already experiencing significantly higher rates of prejudice than any other group in Australia based on blackness as a visible marker of difference (Markus, 2016), Moomba saw a further increase in the number of reports of everyday racism against Sudanese and South Sudanese Australians. This exposure not only harmed the settlement efforts of the Sudanese and South Sudanese communities in Melbourne but also significantly fractured social cohesion within Melbourne suburbs. Inside the South Sudanese community, members described feeling under surveillance, unsafe in public places, vilified and discriminated against in schools and uncertain about their employment prospects (Benier et al., 2018; Henriques-Gomes, 2018; Macaulay & Deppeler, 2020). Similarly, mothers described the impact of their youth being criminalised in the media as well as having their parenting efficacy questioned and overt racism causing distinct changes in their everyday lives (Maher et al., 2020). Across Melbourne's suburbs, sentiments towards Africans became less favourable, with recent empirical evidence showing that low feelings of warmth towards Africans were associated with greater perceptions of problems in the suburbs (Benier et al., 2020). Given that refugee settlement requires a two-way process of mutual understanding of cultural expectations between the host and incoming refugee communities (Abur & Spaaij, 2016), as well as a need for the wider community to adapt to accommodate refugees, it is perhaps unsurprising that the media and political attention created severe problems in relation to belonging, identity and integration for the South Sudanese community.

Stigma, Labelling and Profiling

Before the events of Moomba, Sudanese and South Sudanese immigrants living in Australia were already the target of prejudice, racism and negative attitudes from the general public. A substantial body of research into this demonstrates the difficult lived experiences for refugees from the African continent in navigating a new cultural and social structure that has not always welcomed them (see, for example, Abur & Spaaij, 2016; Dawes et al., 2014; Khan & Pedersen, 2010; Majavu, 2017). This research highlights the existing difficulties faced by South Sudanese families in obtaining meaningful education and employment, accessing support services and feeling a sense of belonging and inclusion within Australian society.

It is clear that the local and national media's ongoing sensationalist and heavily racialised coverage of criminal incidents involving young people 'of African appearance' (see Benier et al., 2018, pp. 8–9) was of further detriment to this group. The media's unrelenting focus on Moomba and the so-called 'Apex gangs' fed underlying implicit and explicit biases related to the perceived association between skin colour and crime. The most problematic aspect of the media coverage was the labelling of all South Sudanese Australians (and indeed anyone from the African continent) as one. This action of labelling an entire group based on the actions of a few resulted in a significant misrepresentation of the majority of South Sudanese Australians in Victoria. In turn, this led to increased racism, which impacted the entire community through their interactions with schools, police and the (white) public. In particular, the constant presence of Africans in the media reaffirmed pre-existing stereotypes that drew on an association between dark skin colour and criminal activity. Often, this resulted in an increased awareness of the presence of people with a South Sudanese background in public space because of society's heightened fear of being a victim of 'African crime'. It is therefore not surprising that South Sudanese Australians have reported increased surveillance of their public lives around the time of Moomba and the so-called African gangs crisis (Benier et al., 2018). For example, with the perception of 'inevitable' criminal activity in shops, store staff often increased surveillance in their store, such as by following South Sudanese people around, or excluded them from the store by asking them to leave. The young people in this study had also been verbally abused, and in some cases physically assaulted, while using public transport (Benier et al., 2018). Comparable experiences were reported by South Sudanese mothers, who experienced similar negative reactions to their presence, including rudeness, fearfulness, passive aggression and staring (Maher et al., 2020). These mothers reported concern for both themselves and their children in facing such treatment. For example, one mother stated:

> Now, when I go shopping centre here, now it's changed. Every time you go, before long, years ago, no one was been check on you, but now everybody look … when they see you, they shocked … They say we are gang whether the woman or man or grandmother or grandfather, they are thinking that we are gangs. This word is killing us as a family. Our kid are not gang. African are not gang. … I'm sorry, our skin is a victim in this country, and we cannot change our skin. We are proud of our skin and we are proud where we come from.
>
> (Maher et al., 2020, p. 8)

It is not only informal surveillance that increased in the aftermath of Moomba but also formal mechanisms of social control. One key consequence of the aftermath of Moomba that had an impact on South Sudanese Australians was an increase in police attention, as detailed in Chapter 4. Racial profiling has been identified as an issue for African Australians in Victoria in recent times, with a landmark Federal Court race discrimination case led by the Flemington and Kensington Community Legal Centre in 2013 (see *Haile-Michael v Konstantinidis* (No 3), 2013). In *Haile-Michael*, Victoria Police settled out of court to avoid a trial over claims of racially profiling young African Australians in Flemington, Melbourne. One outcome of this case was the release of a Victoria Police report, titled *Equality is not the same*, alongside the organisation developing a three-year action plan to review training and policing practices in order to address concerns about discriminatory policing and racial profiling (Victoria Police, 2013). In 2014, officers at Sunshine Police Station in the Western suburbs of Melbourne had their employment terminated and others faced disciplinary action over the production of stubby holders bearing a racist cartoon and language that was derogatory towards African Australians (Donelly, 2014). However, after Moomba, it appears that racial profiling by Victoria Police intensified, with the effect that police encroachment on young people's freedom of movement was unrestrained (Benier et al., 2018).

The increase in the level of police contact further amplified stereotypes as the (majority white) public observed the police questioning and stopping African youths, reaffirming their perception that these young people were dangerous and unruly and frequently engaged in unlawful behaviour. The young people in this research expressed anger, disbelief and dismay at this police discrimination. Despite these young people employing coping strategies such as the use of humour when recounting their stories to others (Benier et al., 2018), this sense of humour did not disguise the hurt and humiliation they felt when being publicly belittled, or the powerlessness that these events caused. Young African people were acutely aware of the use of surveillance targeting their movements in public and at community events and deemed this surveillance to be inappropriate and intimidating, as well as disproportionate to the (low) likelihood of crime and disorder occurring. Mothers also noted this awareness of increased police attention, describing situations in which they feared that their children would have contact with police as a result of police misinterpreting a social group of young people as constituting a 'gang' (Maher et al., 2020).

While teachers and schools are sometimes viewed as a support system for young people experiencing difficulties (Baak, 2019; Cassity & Gow, 2005), our interviews with South Sudanese young people revealed the opposite effect after the #Africangangs attention (Benier et al., 2018). Young African people felt that their classroom and schoolyard experiences of racialised bullying were amplified as a result of the phenomenon. While many reported upsetting interactions with peers, such as teasing, bullying and name-calling, participants also noted that their exchanges with teachers were reinforcing damaging stereotypes. These stereotypes often revolved around academic ability, with South Sudanese young people commenting that teachers often insisted on singling them out in class to offer additional assistance when it was unwarranted, constantly asking if they understood and suggesting that these students should select easier subjects to ensure that they were able to pass the school units. These students felt this differential treatment to be problematic because it visibly reinforces and validates the idea that South Sudanese students are inherently less capable than their non-South Sudanese peers. Further, participants described how the media's reporting of the Apex phenomenon prompted teachers to perceive groups of 'African' students as a risk in relation to school behavioural conduct and to police them accordingly. This further reinforced harmful stereotypes about young South Sudanese students through the school proactively monitoring and policing their behaviour outside the classroom. This heightened surveillance and differential treatment by teachers and schools reaffirmed to the South Sudanese students that they required special treatment and were distinct from their peers and also reinforced their difference and lack of ability compared to non-African students. Such perceptions have a negative impact on South Sudanese young people's sense of belonging within Australian communities by reinforcing their difference.

Family Relationships and Conflict between Generations

One of the most troubling impacts of the 'African gangs' phenomenon was the tension it created in relationships between young African people and their parents. While parents felt that their efficacy – already challenged by a post-settlement context – was threatened by the labelling and criminalisation of young people (Maher et al., 2020), young people reported frustration that their parents would listen to media reports and consequently began to distrust their children instead of supporting them (Benier et al., 2018). This implication is perhaps unsurprising, given that Ali (2008) suggests that parents who migrate from poor countries to developed countries lose their sense of self-efficacy in their parenting role due to a sudden reduction in their social, emotional, cultural and financial resources. This self-doubt, combined with the interactions of migrant families with the social institutions of the countries in which they settle, often perpetuates parents' sense of inadequacy, inferiority and lack of personal efficacy.

Renzaho et al. (2011) found parents from African migrant communities in Australia to be particularly restrictive when their children sought levels of independence that did not reflect those of children in Africa. The resultant parenting styles discouraged children's autonomy, emphasised hierarchical decision-making within the family and attempted to control children's social development and behaviour through strict boundary setting and close monitoring of friends, activities and interests (Renzaho et al., 2011). Further, Hebbani et al. (2009) found that Sudanese mothers felt that their children had abandoned their heritage for an Australian identity and, in doing so, had undermined their mother's authoritative role in their lives and ability to influence their children's social development. These insecurities were further exacerbated by the media and political attention, which emphasised that South Sudanese youth were seen to be violent, uncontrollable and disrespectful to other people, property and police. These mothers worried about the reactions of family members in their homeland, believing that they would be judged as having failed to raise their children properly and appropriately in Australia, just as they believed that Australian society was judging them.

The secondary stigma experienced during this 'law and order crisis' was clearly distressing and a source of anxiety for South Sudanese mothers (Maher et al., 2020). While they acknowledged that their children were torn between belonging to two sometimes opposing cultures, there was frustration that parents' attempts at imposing discipline were often ignored. Many parents attributed their loss of parental authority and control to their children's intercultural identity, alongside government interventions in family functioning by police, schools and child protection agencies. In particular, women identified child protection interventions as causing serious damage to family and community life and to their roles as mothers (Maher, 2018). Further, many mothers often lacked the educational background, cultural knowledge and social capital required to help their children overcome challenges (Maher et al., 2020). As a result, their efforts centred on promoting responsible behaviour and increasing supervision of and support for their children, employing strategies oriented towards preventing the children from making decisions that could jeopardise their futures. While it appears that the South Sudanese mothers in this study seemingly accepted that misbehaving was normal for adolescents in Australia, they believed that the risks and consequences were greater for South Sudanese teenagers due to their visibility and the heightened scrutiny and surveillance that they faced after Moomba. Adolescent deviance was seen as a privilege that young people from the South Sudanese community were not afforded.

Many mothers noted that a lack of employment opportunities, thought to be a result of prejudice and stereotyping, was harming their children's likelihood of success and leading to young people's frustration. This often caused the young people to lose hope, internalising the labelling stigma and choosing to socialise with friends instead of using their time productively. For example, one mother stated:

> Some of them are frustrated because they couldn't get jobs. They struggle and then, what do they do? They end up just loitering around or finding themselves idle, and they end up doing such kind of – it encourages them to do such a kind of behaviours, or drinking. And then, when you're drunk, what does it mean? You start doing other things, which you didn't plan to do. Obviously, later on, you regret, but – yeah. But if the possibility of really getting jobs and they're kept busy, I think they will not have time to be messing around, trying to do such kind of things.
> (Maher et al., 2020, p. 10)

This quote illustrates the frustration experienced by mothers, which was compounded by the intense and persistent attention from political and media sources.

Impacts on Belonging and Identity

The increased attention, negative sentiments and prejudiced attitudes directed at members of the Sudanese and South Sudanese communities have had a significant impact on aspects of their daily lives in Australia, such as through increased surveillance and difficulties at school, as discussed above. Accompanied by the political and media attention emerging from the Moomba events were much broader impacts of this negative attention for individuals, families and communities in the form of damage to their sense of belonging, limitations on their future opportunities and challenges to their sense of identity.

The importance of social bonds for an individual's mental and physical health, as well as for social cohesion within the neighbourhood, has been well established for some time (Longshore et al., 2005; Ryan et al., 2008; Sampson & Laub, 1990). Indeed, many studies highlight the importance of forming and maintaining social bonds for survival, while some detail the mental and physical health repercussions of neglecting to form interpersonal attachments and being socially rejected (for more detail, see Lambert et al., 2013). Belonging implies feeling 'at home' and being emotionally attached to one's place of residence and community (Yuval-Davis, 2006, 2011). For Sudanese and South Sudanese Australian youth, belonging can be supported by enhanced health and wellbeing (Correa-Velez et al., 2010), positive education experiences (Cassity & Gow, 2005) and multicultural friendship networks (Collins et al., 2011). Identity forming through place-making has also been described as significant in influencing the wellbeing of young South Sudanese people (Sampson & Gifford, 2010). Yet, for one to belong in a multi-cultural context, members of the majority population must 'grant' that belonging to the minority groups (Hopkins, 2011; Spaaij, 2015). People achieve a sense of belonging by feeling that they can express their own identity, feel valued and listened to and be recognised as an integral part of the community.

The post-Moomba environment for the Sudanese and South Sudanese communities appeared to be one in which the general Australian population, as a whole, are unwilling to 'grant' belonging or offer acceptance to this community in the wake of media-fuelled social divisions that have excluded the Sudanese and South Sudanese from the broader Melbourne community. Some members of the South Sudanese community have spent most of their lives as residents in Victoria yet reported that it still does not feel like home (Benier et al., 2018). One of the most common emotions experienced by the South Sudanese community was a sense of isolation and a lack of community connectedness (Abur & Mphande, 2020; Abur & Spaaij, 2016). This is reflected in research by Henriques-Gomes (2018), who cites an interviewee in his research as stating that

> ...we feel like we don't have any back-up in this country ... If even the prime minister uses us as a shield to win votes, who can we go to?.

Another point of frustration that emerged in the aftermath of Moomba and the 'African gangs' phenomenon for South Sudanese people was the public's cultural ignorance when it came to the social dynamics of different Sudanese and South Sudanese communities. Participants in a study by Benier and colleagues (2018) felt that many Australians had little appreciation of the differences between the (various) African and Australian cultures. In their view, any behaviour is interpreted by the general public according to the lens of the dominant Australian culture, especially family functioning. As such, participants stated that the prevalence of strict parenting practices, common in many South Sudanese communities (see Deng, 2017), is often unknown to the public and therefore has not helped to counteract the media's portrayal of young South Sudanese Australians as lacking parental supervision and positive role models. Similarly, there was frustration among the participants that the strong emphasis on socialisation and peer and family association within many African cultures was not understood by the non-African community. For example, kinship is an important element of African community and it is rare to see an individual walking down the street alone. However, the general public views these clusters of African people as a threat to law and order rather than a point of cultural difference. The lack of understanding within media reports, evident in the grouping of all Africans into one cultural category, without recognising the large number of different countries, cultures, diasporas and communities that comprise the African continent, was another source of frustration.

Despite Australia priding itself on the diversity of its residents and highlighting its multiculturalism as a strength on the world stage (Dunn, 2004), the reality is that Australia has current and historic problems with prejudice, stereotyping and racism. Experiences of discrimination based on appearance mean that young people often feel that, in order to belong, they must comply, adapt or 'fit in' with 'white' Australian culture (Benier et al., 2018). There is a perception among immigrants that there is no acceptance of different cultures within Australian society, despite people appreciating the idea of multiculturalism in theory (Dandy & Pe-Pua, 2010). Over the past 50 years of immigration, Australians have generally been supportive of certain types of immigrants, such as European skilled workers, while being reluctant to accept humanitarian visa holders from Asian, Middle Eastern or African countries (Arasaratnam, 2014; Benier & Corcoran, 2018; Markus et al., 2009). These attitudes have been exacerbated by the negative attention on African immigrants which has heightened a fear of difference among the white majority population. For example, one young person in a study by Benier et al. (2018, p. 32) stated:

> Like, Australia has this term, we're a 'multiculture', but they're not in reality. In reality, if you're not white, you're beneath us. They just use the term 'multiculture' so it makes them look good. And when they do it, they take the good out of Sudanese culture – when they're doing well: 'You know what? They Sudanese Australian'. But as soon as someone does one thing bad, 'Ugh, sorry, you're African. You don't belong here'.

It is not surprising that the South Sudanese community has expressed cynical attitudes about the lived reality of multiculturalism in Australia. In particular, Benier et al. (2018) found that South Sudanese young people believed that distinct markers of difference and discrimination depended on the context of the situation. They felt that in a positive situation, such as a news story on the success of an African (a story of heroism, a successful AFL or basketball player, or someone doing well in their career), the community was happy to embrace multiculturalism and referred to the individual as a Sudanese Australian. However, in stories of crime and disorder, or other negative portrayals, the public was quick to refer to the individual as something like 'a young African migrant refugee from a South Sudanese background' (Benier et al., 2018, p. 32). Within this discriminatory system, participants in this study felt that the label 'Australian' was used to describe positive qualities and positive contributions to society. In the case of immigrants, the implication is that, by being successful or doing good things, they are exhibiting 'Australianness'. Conversely, participants felt that the cause of a wrongdoing by an African Australian was rarely attributed to Australian culture, policies, institutions or systemic barriers to social inclusion. Instead, it was attributed to the 'Africanness' of the perpetrator. In other words, blame is located in their perceived inability to adapt, rather than their alleged wrongdoing being framed as a consequence of their efforts to belong being blocked by cultural, structural, political and systemic barriers. This social distancing by the majority population has made it difficult for the South Sudanese community as their perceived degree of 'belonging' has varied – subject to change based on the current news stories of the time. One of the most poignant observations from a South Sudanese young woman was as follows:

> There are times we belong here, and there are times that we don't.
> And it's just, we don't want to not belong here, and we don't want
> to belong here only when we're doing positive things. We want to
> belong here no matter what.
>
> (Benier et al., 2018, p. 33)

Identity is defined as 'narratives, stories that people tell themselves about who they are, who they are not, as well as who and how they would like to/should be' (Yuval-Davis, 2010, p. 266). Immigrant identity is primarily determined by a sense of belonging in a new cultural environment, with formation occurring through place-making (Sampson & Gifford, 2010; Schwartz et al., 2006). Some young people from the South Sudanese community in Australia have actively attempted to dissociate themselves from their community as a means of avoiding negative stereotypes (Benier et al., 2018). This permits them to find a place in society that engenders less conflict and tension for them, a place that perhaps allows them to develop a hybrid identity, which in turn decreases the level of negative public attention upon them (Benier et al., 2018). In contrast, some of these young people protect themselves by turning inwards, aligning more strongly with the South Sudanese community under the guise of protection in numbers. For South Sudanese women, the events of Moomba have challenged their identity as mothers in Australian society and undermined their parental authority. For some, that sense has been significantly damaged or irreplaceably destroyed (Maher et al., 2020).

Belonging and identity also manifest through opportunities, both economic and social or cultural (Losoncz, 2011, 2017). Many African community leaders point to high levels of unemployment as a key factor driving the problems affecting this small minority of young people (Henriques-Gomes, 2018). Employment is not only a pathway out of poverty and insecurity but also pro-vides opportunities to interact with other Australians and learn more about Australian culture and society, as well as enabling social connectedness. This leads to an increased sense of integration and inclusion. In 2011, the unemploy-ment rate in the South Sudanese population was six times higher than the national average (Losoncz, 2017). As of 2018, the unemployment rate for Sudan-born people above the age of 15 was 25.4%, according to the Department of Social Services (Henriques-Gomes, 2018). This suggests that there are limited opportu-nities for casual or professional employment for Sudanese and South Sudanese Australians (El-Gack & Yak, 2016).

> People want to work, but it's very difficult for them to get a job. And then the Centrelink pressure and stress for them to get the job, it's really very stressful and most people are really depressed, they are sleepless because, 'Oh my god, tomorrow they're going to ask me'. What about if they stop the money? How am I going to stay in my home, especially when you have children? ... All that fear, it's not good that the people are restless because of that condition.
>
> (Maher, 2018, p. 153)

Despite some stories of Sudanese and South Sudanese Australians succeeding in high-profile careers and sports, many may feel that they must work harder than others to access opportunities and constantly prove themselves, especially in the wake of negative media representations. In particular, the young people in our study felt that they had to 'prove that you're more than your colour' (Benier et al., 2018, p. 35). The perception of opportunities being blocked in this way has created frustration, suspicion, disappointment, concern for siblings and feelings of being judged and labelled (Benier et al., 2018). Several studies have found that people avoid using traditional or South Sudanese names on their résumés to increase their likelihood of receiving a follow-up interview (Benier et al., 2018; Henriques-Gomes, 2018).

Given the extensive impact of the political and media coverage on the Sudanese and South Sudanese lived experience in Australia, it is not surprising that South Sudanese young people and their parents in our empirical research feel exhausted, powerless and worn down. Young people stressed that while they wanted to fight back to defend themselves, to prove that they are 'more than their colour' (Benier et al., 2018, p. 35), the fight was just too big to tackle. Thus, it quickly became overwhelming, particularly for the young people who were already navigating a tricky time of development in their lives, adolescence. With adolescence constituting a critical period for identity formation, the impact of being constantly devalued and told that they are unworthy of acceptance in Australia is significant and highly detrimental.

Reactions from the Broader Community

Despite the ethnic diversification that has occurred over the past several decades, scholarship continues to demonstrate that being black in Australia hinders social acceptance (Ndhlovu, 2013) and can be a disadvantaging social factor (Colic-Peisker & Tilbury, 2008). Empirical and anecdotal evidence suggests that the so-called 'law and order crisis' in 2016 exacerbated existing prejudice within the broader community. Specifically, Majavu (2020, p. 27) emphasises that media reporting throughout this time provided 'a good example that illustrates how the long-standing racist trope of conflating blackness with criminality is employed in Australia'. While it is certainly not uncommon for this connection to be drawn in any context (Benier et al., 2020), we argue that such attention has further fractured social inclusion within Australian communities by portraying Sudanese and South Sudanese people as 'folk devils'. Chapter 4 illustrates how the media reported that police were hesitant to control young people for fear of racism complaints (see also MacDonald, 2017) and that South Sudanese youth did not respect police officers or Australian law. These two factors led the general majority population to believe that youth crime within this population was uncontrollable. In turn, Sudanese and South Sudanese people were actively excluded from the broader community through overt racism that was encouraged by less warmth and more anger towards the group.

It is clear from the literature that African migrants in Australia experience high levels of racial discrimination (Australian Law Reform Commission, 2018; Baak, 2019; Majavu, 2018, 2020; Udah, 2018). This has been felt particularly in and across neighbourhoods, with African migrants reporting that Australian neighbourhood life is unfriendly, unwelcoming and alienating (Majavu, 2017). Despite no evidence of actual gang activity in the aftermath of Moomba, the backlash against black migrants in Melbourne has led to increases in reported racism and institutionalised forms of discrimination. In a neighbourhood study of Melbourne, Wickes and colleagues (2020) explored the context of racial and cultural exclusivism. Their study was conducted in 2017, during the peak of the crisis, when public attitudes were likely to have been impacted by the ongoing focus on African migrants. The results from the study suggest that a sizeable number of participants felt anger and little warmth towards African people (Wickes et al., 2020). Specifically, nearly one in four participants (24.9%) reported experiencing little warmth towards people of African heritage, and approximately one in six (16.31%) participants reported a significant level of anger directed at people of African heritage. Further breakdown of these responses highlighted a correlation with age, with older survey participants more likely to report negative sentiments towards the group.

These results align strongly with the findings of our focus groups with South Sudanese young people. In a study on the effects of the Moomba riot, Benier and colleagues (2018) identified that the attention had rendered overt forms of racism directed at South Sudanese Australians more socially acceptable, with participants stating that the media gave the public the 'power to ... abuse' and 'the confidence to make assumptions' (p. 19). That is, the media saturation of studies about 'African gangs' and 'Apex' crime played a role in validating and arguably normalising pre-existing racist stereotypes among some people within the Victorian population. These racist and xenophobic views were visible not only in the everyday interactions with the general public but also on social media. Exemplary here are the following Facebook comments made in response to a news story about alleged gang activity.

> And then when I go into a comments section on Facebook, for example, like and it's, like, all of a sudden all of these people, who had problems with African youth, Sudanese people, they just emerged out of nowhere and it just seemed like the whole wider community were on the same page. There was not a single person, like on our side trying to defend and say, 'Okay, it's not all of them there'. It's just everyone agreeing, 'Oh, send them back'. Um, 'These dogs, deport them', and all these things. So, the

> comments really hurt me more than when I saw the photos, so
> that's what I can remember from the media coverage of Moomba.
> (Benier et al., 2018, p. 19)

Such comments acted as a constant reminder that the South Sudanese community was perceived as 'different' to the Australian public because they were deemed to lack respect for others, the police and Australian laws. Comments often suggested tougher immigration policies and the use of deportation for alleged offenders to reduce recidivism and encourage others to desist from offending.

The 'othering' created by a racial dichotomy between black and white further distances the African community from white Australians, many of whom perceive the African migrant as a threat to national homogeneity. Using the aforementioned data from Wickes and colleagues (2020), Benier et al. (2020) examined the impact of the 'African gangs' media coverage on the development of anti-African sentiments in Melbourne following the Moomba incident. Their findings clearly demonstrate that both anger towards Africans and political preference have become strongly linked to the (white majority) public's perceptions of increased community problems in their own suburbs. Interestingly, it was also identified that negative contact with Africans was associated with increased perceptions of community problems, although neutral or positive contact did not alter people's perceptions. This finding stands in contrast to a significant body of literature that shows the benefits of meaningful contact between in-groups and out-groups (see, for example, Pettigrew & Tropp, 2006; Zhou et al., 2019). This may be because there is already a deeply embedded bias in Australia that links being black with problems of crime and delinquency (Majavu, 2020; Mapedzahama & Kwansah-Aidoo, 2017). These pre-existing uncertainties, combined with the extensive and harmful media and political rhetoric surrounding the Moomba riot, have likely impeded the benefits that usually follow from positive contact.

Conclusion

Without a doubt, the most detrimental outcome of the 'law and order crisis' in Melbourne was harm to the Sudanese and South Sudanese communities. The prolific media and political attention around African communities traumatised an already-marginalised population by increasing social distance, heightening the racial divide and exacerbating pre-existing prejudice. Impacts were particularly profound for the young South Sudanese people in our research who experienced such exclusion and included diminished self-esteem and self-confidence, which is particularly challenging in these formative years. It is likely that these consequences will have ongoing effects for their sense of identity and belonging for years to come. Settings that often offer support in the tumultuous teenage years, such as peers and school settings, have instead caused greater damage. Further, parents – particularly mothers – have been forced to question their authority and ability to control their children, second-guessing their decisions and unable to find the support they need in this new cultural context. The social divide created by the 'African gangs' phenomenon was not only responsible for the direct exclusion of Sudanese and South Sudanese people but also heightened community divisions more broadly. In a country that has historical tensions between racial groups, this is a social convention that can be ill afforded.

Chapter 6

Conclusion: The Anatomy of a Law and Order Crisis

In 2015, there was a noticeable spike in violent crimes committed by a small number of young people in Melbourne (Victorian Ombudsman, 2017, p. 2).[1] Some of these young people were African Australian or of South Sudanese heritage, yet most were from a range of other national and ethnic backgrounds. An adequate investigation into these young people's offending patterns and the complex interplay of the proximate and distal factors driving them would require a book of its own. We have produced a very different book, which proceeds from the observation that, notwithstanding the 'law and order crisis' over 'African gangs', the face of violent crime in Melbourne remains overwhelmingly 'non-African', in that the majority of people charged with crimes against the person (including burglary, assault, robbery and affray) are Australian-born (Goldsworthy, 2018). The question, then, is how and why a relatively newly arrived group of Melburnians came to be identified as a unique threat to community safety?

The answer, we believe, rests in the process through which the physical and cultural difference of this relatively new migrant group has been translated into perceptions of threat and viewed through the prism of danger (Lianos & Douglas, 2000). The arguments and empirical research presented in this book have dissected the main elements of this 'crisis' to reveal its underlying anatomy. We have shown how this occurred through the ongoing racialised and stigmatising representation of African Australians in public discourse – particularly through the media – as dangerous 'others' incapable of integrating into Australian life. Within this narrative, the extreme economic marginalisation, intergenerational trauma and systemic discrimination experienced by Sudanese and South Sudanese humanitarian migrants have been largely erased, so that any apparent difficulties arising from the settlement process can be attributed not to shortcomings in government support or a lack of community acceptance but to the so-called failures of African communities themselves.

While acknowledging the broader socioeconomic circumstances, we have argued that this process has been largely politically driven. At a state level, we

---

[1]Children's Court sentencing data show a corresponding increase in the number of children receiving custodial sentences in the years 2015–2018 (Sentencing Advisory Council, 2021).

Place, Race and Politics, 103–108
Copyright © 2021 Leanne Weber, Jarrett Blaustein, Kathryn Benier, Rebecca Wickes and Diana Johns
Published under exclusive licence by Emerald Publishing Limited
doi:10.1108/978-1-80043-045-720211006

have shown that the media-fuelled 'crisis' was stoked largely by conservative opposition politicians seeking to gain electoral advantage in the lead-up to the 2018 Victorian election by misrepresenting and exaggerating the disturbances that occurred at the 2016 Moomba Festival. This took place against a backdrop of rising nationalism and authoritarianism at the federal level, which contrasts with the continued commitment to multiculturalism espoused at the state level. In line with the governmental practices identified by Franko (2020) in relation to those who are putatively identified as 'crimmigrants', the state government in Victoria focussed its critique on a subgroup of wrongdoers, rather than on the African Australian community as a whole, enabling the government to demonstrate a broader public commitment to the multicultural project.

One way of understanding why the 'law and order crisis' following Moomba 2016 fixated on South Sudanese Australians as a unique threat to community safety is through the prism of risk and dangerisation. Within the context of late modern neoliberal capitalism, in a society shaped by liberal democratic values and individualistic notions of success and responsibility, structural failings tend to be individualised, with particular groups frequently blamed and responsibilised for wider social problems (Bauman, 2013). When widespread anxieties – such as perceptions of rising youth violence and a youth justice system in crisis – combine with the smouldering suspicion of a group seen as outsiders (recall Federal Immigration Minister Kevin Andrews's 2007 comments about the failure of Sudanese communities to integrate 'into the Australian way of life'), these converging currents upwell into a pervasive sense of threat. The 'good society' – to which 'we' (of this diverse multicultural community) ostensibly all belong – becomes the touchstone for identifying risks to safety from 'others' who appear not to belong, and whose 'difference and otherness can only be established in terms of dangerousness' (Lianos & Douglas, 2000, p. 267). Racism is rinsed through the language of integration and social cohesion.[2] The power of this process was first apparent in the bizarre response in some quarters to the racist murder of South Sudanese teenager Liep Gony in 2007, in which he was presented as the problem, rather than the white supremacists who killed him. Dangerisation thus preserves Australians' sense of themselves as 'inclusive' and 'tolerant' while legitimising racist othering in the name of securitisation. At the time of Moomba 2016, against this normative and discursive background, the idea of the dangerous other took embodied form in 'South Sudanese youth', whose supposed dangerousness was epitomised by the mythologised 'Apex gang'.

While this messaging seemed to have an impact on some Melbourne residents, one of the young people who participated in our research pointed out the fallacy of representing any migrant community as posing a unique and insurmountable threat:

---

[2]'Having a more equal focus across Africa, the Middle East and Asia hardly constitutes "racism." Australia has the right to ensure that those who come here are integrating into a socially cohesive community' (Federal Immigration Minister Kevin Andrews quoted by Pearlman, 5 October 2007).

How long have Sudanese been in Australia? Not long, man. How long have criminals been in Australia? Way longer … We've had different sorts of immigrants, we've had the Greeks, we had the Islanders, we had the Italians, the Vietnamese, the Cambodians. All of them have come in, had their problems. As if this is new. They're acting like this is new, bro. That's such a sin.

Other young people who participated in our research explicitly called out the media for what they perceived to be its role in constructing racialised narratives about 'Apex' and 'African gangs'.

And the media, it's all about finances for them. It's all about money. It's not really about. … It's all propaganda. Whatever. They say whatever comes. Like, whatever comes to their table, the media, like, like blow it up. That's how they make money. That's how they make a living.[3]

Journalists' motivations for reporting on this story are complex and varied (Koumouris & Blaustein, 2021), but our analysis in Chapter 3 evidences that the mainstream media played an active and crucial role in co-constructing, validating and amplifying the visibility of this supposed threat through familiar narratives about Black, migrant criminality in Australia. Conservative newspapers that formed part of the Murdoch stable evidently played a leading role in promoting this narrative, but the issue also received widespread coverage in other centrist and left-leaning outlets.

It is also clear from our analysis in Chapter 4 that Victoria Police occupied a pivotal position in relation to the 'African gangs' crisis. On the one hand, it responded at both the local and strategic levels to community fears whipped up by the overblown media discourse and the public expectations this generated, including by implementing a range of non-punitive interventions. On the other hand, its practices at the local and strategic levels sometimes singled out African Australians as a uniquely threatening group. At the street level, these practices included the breaking up of gatherings of young people – which potentially played into broader fears about the existence of 'street gangs' – and the racialised targeting of young people of African appearance within these groups, which identified them as particular threats and placed them at the pinnacle of a 'hierarchy of discrimination'. At the strategic level, the implementation of a special African Australian Community Taskforce, while seemingly intended to reduce the recourse to punitive intervention, also publicly defined this section of the community as a unique problem and as responsible for their own predicament. While statements made to the media by senior police and officers at the local level were somewhat mixed, police practices on the ground also communicated powerful messages directly to the wider community. This contributed to a 'politics of

---

[3]This quote also appears in Benier, Blaustein, Johns, and Maher (2018, p. 18).

belonging' (Yuval-Davis, 2011) in which African Australian young people were cast as dangerous outsiders.

We observed through our local-level research how risk-based approaches aimed at identifying 'youth network offenders' seemed to be driving high levels of contact between police and young African Australians, even though race and ethnicity were said not to feature in the algorithms used in the risk-based systems applied by local police. Even in the absence of formal policy, the high levels of surveillance to which this group was subjected, and the growing threat of permanent exclusion through deportation, could be traced to an attribution of 'crimmigrant status' (Franko, 2020) that played out in everyday policing. We were able to observe all the elements identified by Franko as common responses to criminalised others who lack the protection of citizenship: namely intensive surveillance, the application of penal power and, ultimately, physical exclusion through deportation.

While local police are the initial gatekeepers to the system of deportation on character grounds, federal government policies also facilitate this exclusionary outcome for young people deemed to be 'crimmigrants'. The guidelines for the cancellation of visas by immigration officials on character grounds list membership of 'violent youth gangs' in the highest risk category, alongside convictions for organised child exploitation, murder and crimes against humanity. Indeed, mere membership of one of these gangs, which may be based solely, it would seem, on police allegations, is considered such a threat to national security that it must be dealt with personally by the Minister for Home Affairs. Although African Australians would not be the only target for this extraordinary measure, this embedding within the immigration system of a seemingly disproportionate response to gang membership indicates the wide-ranging ramifications of the law and order crisis over 'African gangs' at both the local and federal level.

As highlighted in Chapter 5, another consequence of sustained media and political attention on the allegedly violent nature of South Sudanese young people's engagement in criminal activity was the exacerbation of pre-existing prejudice and stereotyping within the broader community. The conflation of blackness with criminality in Australia, as in other developed nations, is certainly not a new phenomenon. However, Moomba and its aftermath, which saw the active exclusion of cultural groups who represent the 'other', led to increased social isolation for a group that was already marginalised. This was evidenced by data from the neighbourhood study by Wickes et al. (2020), in which one in four survey participants reported low levels of warmth towards people of African heritage and one in six respondents reported high feelings of anger towards people of African heritage. According to the young people in our research, consistent media saturation and political attention gave (white majority) community members the confidence to outwardly display the prejudice and racism that had previously remained silenced. With South Sudanese communities reporting that the general community sentiment towards them was unfriendly, unwelcoming and alienating, a biased media and political narrative that enabled and further cemented these notions was clearly detrimental.

Sustained exposure to the criminalising discourse around 'African gangs' has taken a significant toll on the wellbeing of South Sudanese Australians, in particular. The serious social, emotional and practical impacts of these events have been clearly articulated through opinion pieces authored by leading commentators from within African Australian communities.[4] In addition to this commentary on the impacts of the 'law and order crisis' on the communities targeted by these events, we do not claim to speak on their behalf. Rather, we have attempted to convey the experiences and concerns that were expressed to us by community members in the course of multiple studies.

Young people from across the South Sudanese community felt shamed and stigmatised and reported heightened perceptions and experiences of racism and discrimination in all aspects of life. Parents and community leaders also reported heightened anxieties about both the wellbeing of young people in their community and the reputational damage that the 'African gangs crisis' had inflicted on the South Sudanese Australian community. Our study into young South Sudanese Australians' interactions with police found that being singled out for unwarranted police attention had a profound effect, both on trust in police and more broadly in terms of feelings of safety, acceptance and belonging. Both younger and older community members reported feeling unprotected by police, with one South Sudanese Australian woman noting that 'police are good for some people but not for us'.

Young people in our studies reported feeling anxious about unwanted police contact, which they experienced in shopping centres, at train stations and when simply walking home from social and sporting events. They often expressed the view that avoiding going out in public was the only way to keep safe, although they were not necessarily prepared to do so. This represents a severe impediment to the capacity of young people to participate freely in community life, which one youth worker described as being forced to 'tiptoe around'. The South Sudanese Australian mothers who spoke with us also expressed deep-seated fears that their children would be harmed or criminalised as a result of interactions with police over which they had no control. While personal experiences are likely to differ by age, gender and across class divides, the research canvassed in this book suggests that the effects of the 'African gangs' crisis in Melbourne have been felt across the whole community.

Our research also highlighted the resilience of the South Sudanese community in the face of these damaging narratives. It is not our intention to present a deterministic account of the stigmatising effects of the 'crisis' and its impact on future offending behaviour by members of the South Sudanese community. At the same time, the long-term consequences of this experience for this community are, as yet, unclear and we can only hope that these labelling processes do not serve to exacerbate and reproduce systemic issues that contribute to social and material

---

[4]For an insider perspective on the 'African gangs' discourse and its community and political impact, see, for example, Santilla Chingaipe (2017), Nyadol Nyuon (2018) and Maker Mayek (2018).

disadvantage. Because it is difficult, perhaps impossible, to disentangle the causes of primary offending from the effects of labelling, the full effects of this 'crisis' for the South Sudanese community in terms of their criminalisation may never be known. At any rate, it seems clear to us that locating responsibility for a population's involvement with offending in that community's alleged shortcomings or failures is counterproductive on a number of fronts.

Although the 'crisis' over 'African crime' presented African Australians as a threat to other Melbourne residents, we learned from participants in our research that it was their community that had lost the sense of security they had hoped to find in Australia. Sacrificing the security of one section of the population to promote a semblance of security for the majority is a divisive strategy that substitutes for proactive efforts to promote equality and build the foundations of social harmony. This is what dangerisation looks like: an overwhelmingly law-abiding community is cast as a threat to 'social cohesion' and community safety. Threats to Sudanese/South Sudanese lives and safety are misrepresented as a failure to settle and adjust or a danger to 'the Australian way of life'. South Sudanese Australians' sense of not belonging is defined as *their problem*, rather than a result of racist othering and political demonisation. Their exclusion is constructed as a source of danger to everybody else, rather than a risk to the safety and wellbeing of members of African Australian communities themselves. And all this takes place behind the normative veil of social cohesion and tolerance. This begs the question, if dominant narratives and notions about ourselves as 'the good society' (Hallsworth & Young, 2008) involve being 'tolerant' of difference, who or what is being 'tolerated'? Must there always be an 'other'?

It is fitting to give the last word on the origins and legacy of the 'African gangs' crisis to one of our research participants, a grassroots community worker. She locates the problems faced by her South Sudanese Australian community, not with the community and their inability to integrate, but with a 'crisis' that was not of their making, experienced against a backdrop of neoliberal ideology that prioritises penality and exclusion over community empowerment through the provision of social and economic support.

> When we come here we think we belong here. We are citizens here, not just come and go back. But not anymore because of the crisis created by media and government. The government should treat us as their own people. But they give authority to police more than us ... We are good people. We take care of this country. If this country accommodate us well we need to do something good ... We get no help for us to see what we can do for ourselves. If we have job we will pay tax to help another person.

To conclude, we (writing as non-Indigenous academics) acknowledge that we are occupiers in and on this Country. If we belong here, African Australians belong here too. It is for everyone on this continent to build a culture and community of belonging that holds and sustains us all.

Appendix 1: Refinement of Media Search Strategy

Project Title

Media portrayals of 'African gangs crisis'

Objective

The objective of this search strategy was to examine media reporting around African youth crime. In order to determine the impact of the African gangs phenomenon on the broader community (e.g., general public), we examined what 'information' people were exposed to through various media sources.

Methods

Electronic Searches

Relevant news publications were identified through electronic searches of bibliographic databases, news pages and Internet search engines. This search filtered for reports in English only. The search used Factiva to search the following news sources:

- *Herald Sun*
- *The Age*
- *The Australian*
- *ABC Australia*
- 9NEWS
- *Daily Telegraph*
- SMH – Australian Breaking News
- News.com.au – Australian news site
- *SBS Australia.*

A general web search was also conducted using Google to identify potential reports. The first 50 hits from Google per term and country were screened.

Search Terms

An initial search strategy is listed below. Both subject headings and text words were searched, and news articles collected were selected from Australia as outlined above from 2008 to 08 June 2020 initially.

- Africa* AND Gang
- Australian Africa* AND Gang
- South Sudan* AND Gang
- Sudan* and Gang
- Crime-Wave AND Gang
- Home invasion AND Gang
- Riot AND Gang
- Youth AND Gang
- Apex AND Gang
- Moomba AND Gang
- Community taskforce AND Gang
- African AND Crime
- Australian African AND Crime
- South Sudan* AND Crime
- Sudan* AND Crime
- Riot AND Crime
- Youth AND Crime
- Apex AND Crime
- Moomba
- Community taskforce

Revised Search Strategy

Initially the search with Gang AND (one of the identified terms) returned 17,803 results. After reviewing the first 600 articles, it was evident that the search was capturing articles relating to organised crime in addition to 'African gangs crisis'. As this was not the focus of this analysis the caveat 'NOT bikie' was included in the search. This reduced the search results to 13,094.

The search for Crime AND [one of the identified terms] returned 150,641 results. After reviewing the first 1,000 articles, it was clear that articles returned related to broader crime, producing further irrelevant results. For example:

Nation

Not fair: Andrews China deal is 'one way traffic'

Lachlan Moffet Gray, Sarah Elks

Sarah Elks, Lachlan Moffet Gray

11,043 words

21 May 2020

For this reason the search strategy was reviewed.

(1) Gang AND Crime OR

- Africa*
- Australian Africa*
- South Sudan*
- Sudan*
- Crime-Wave
- Home invasion
- Riot
- Youth
- Apex
- Moomba
- Community taskforce
(2) NOT Bikie*
(3) NOT China
(4) NOT Carl Williams

This resulted in 6,206 results and it was determined as a more accurate search strategy in line with the purposes of the research. Of these, 819 were determined to be identical duplicates by Factiva, leaving 5,387 independent articles to review, which were all downloaded into Word.

After a brief review of a sample of 5,387 articles, a final change to the search terms was made to capture only those articles in line with the goals of the research. These included the following:

(1) Gang AND Crime OR

- Africa*
- 'South Sudanese'
- 'South Sudan'
- Sudan*
- Apex
(2) NOT Bikie*
(3) NOT China
(4) NOT Carl Williams

This refined search resulted in 1,393 results. Of these, 235 were identical duplicates as reported by Factiva. This left *1,158* independent articles as the basis of our analyses. Electronic PDF copies of relevant documents from Internet-based sources were created with the exact URL and date of access.

References

3AWRadio. (2016, March 14). Riot at Federation Square during Moomba festival. *Youtube*. https://www.youtube.com/watch?v=6ucwIq-Ys4Q

ABC News. (2016, July 21). Police, youth experts gather in Melbourne to discuss growing problem of violent gangs. https://www.abc.net.au/news/2016-07-21/police-and-experts-gather-in-melbourne-to-discuss-youth-crime/7647594

ABC News. (2018, January 1). Malcolm Turnbull and Greg Hunt discuss 'African gang crime' in Melbourne. https://www.abc.net.au/news/2018-01-01/malcolm-turnbull-and-greg-hunt-discuss-african/9296708

Abur, W., & Mphande, C. (2020). Mental health and wellbeing of South Sudanese-Australians. *Journal of Asian and African Studies, 55*(3), 412–428.

Abur, W., & Spaaij, R. (2016). Settlement and employment experiences of South Sudanese people from refugee backgrounds in Melbourne, Australia. *Australasian Review of African Studies, 37*(2), 107.

Akerman, T. (2017, December 4). Migrants 'need law lessons to cut crime'. *The Australian*, p. 3.

Alexander, M. (2010). *The new Jim Crow: Mass incarceration in the age of colorblindness*. The New Press.

Ali, M. A. (2008). Loss of parenting self-efficacy among immigrant parents. *Contemporary Issues in Early Childhood, 9*(2), 148–160.

Andrews, D. (2016, December 5). Sweeping reforms to cut down on youth crime [press release]. The Hon Daniel Andrews MP, Premier. Victorian Government.

Andrews, D. [@DanielAndrewsMP] (2016, March 14). For the perpetrators, Saturday night was a choice – And it's one they will regret [Tweet]. *Twitter*. https://twitter.com/DanielAndrewsMP/status/709214154339405824

Andrews, D. (2017, February 6). *Building a stronger and more secure youth justice system*. The Premier of Victoria, Media Release. https://www.premier.vic.gov.au/building-stronger-and-more-secure-youth-justice-system

Arasaratnam, L. A. (2014). A discussion of multiculturalism in Australia from educators' perspective. *SpringerPlus, 3*(1), 1–8.

Armstrong, D. (2004). A risky business? Research, policy, governmentality and youth offending. *Youth Justice, 4*(2), 100–116.

Armytage, P., & Ogloff, J. (2017). *Meeting needs and reducing offending: Youth justice review and strategy – Part 1*. Victorian Government.

Australian Broadcasting Corporation (ABC). (2018, September 5). Fact check: Do Sudanese people account for only 1 per cent of crimes committed in Victoria? https://www.abc.net.au/news/2018-09-05/fact-check-sudanese-gangs-victoria/10187550

Australian Bureau of Statistics (ABS). (2011). *2011 census data*. https://www.abs.gov.au/websitedbs/censushome.nsf/home/historicaldata2011?opendocument&navpos=280

Australian Bureau of Statistics (ABS). (2016). *Australian census 2016*. Australian Bureau of Statistics.

Australian Council of Social Services (ACOSS). (2015). *Inequality in Australia: A nation divided*. http://www.acoss.org.au/wp-content/uploads/2015/06/Inequality_in_Australia_FINAL.pdf

Australian Human Rights Commission. (2010). *In our own words: African Australians – A review of human rights and social inclusion issues*. https://humanrights.gov.au/our-work/race-discrimination/projects/our-own-words-african-australians-review-human-rights-and

Australian Law Reform Commission. (2018). *Pathways to justice: Inquiry into the incarceration rate of Aboriginal and Torres Strait Islander peoples – Disproportionate incarceration rate*. https://www.alrc.gov.au/publication/pathways-to-justice-inquiry-into-the-incarceration-rate-of-aboriginal-and-torres-strait-islander-peoples-alrc-report-133/executive-summary-15/disproportionate-incarceration-rate/

Baak, M. (2019). Racism and othering for South Sudanese heritage students in Australian schools: Is inclusion possible? *International Journal of Inclusive Education, 23*(2), 125–141.

Barker, V. (2009). *The politics of imprisonment: How democratic process shapes the way America punishes offenders*. Oxford University Press.

Bauman, Z. (2000). *Liquid modernity*. Polity Press.

Bauman, Z. (2013). *Collateral damage*. Polity Press.

Baxendale, R. (2018, July 23). African crime a Victorian problem, Alan Tudge says. *The Australian*. Document AUSTOL0020180723ee7n001rx.

Beaumont, A. (2018, November 24). Labor has landslide win in Victoria. *The Conversation*. https://theconversation.com/labor-has-landslide-win-in-victoria-107514

Benier, K. J., Blaustein, J. B., Johns, D., & Maher, S. L. (2018). *'Don't drag us into this': Growing up South Sudanese in Victoria after the 2016 Moomba 'riot'*. Centre for Multicultural Youth. https://www.cmy.net.au/resource/dont-drag-me-into-this-growing-up-south-sudanese-in-victoria-after-the-2016-moomba-riot/

Benier, K., & Corcoran, J. (2018). State of the art and future challenges of interregional migration empirical research in Oceania. In B. Biagi, A. Faggian, I. Rajbhandari, & V. A. Venhorst (Eds.), *New frontiers in interregional migration research* (pp. 125–147). Springer.

Benier, K., Wickes, R., & Moran, C. (2020). 'African gangs' in Australia: Perceptions of race and crime in urban neighbourhoods. *Australian and New Zealand Journal of Criminology, 54*(2), 220–238. https://doi.org/10.1177/0004865820965647

Bigo, D. (2011). Security, exception, ban and surveillance. In D. Lyon (Ed.), *Theorizing surveillance: The panopticon and beyond* (pp. 46–68). Willan Publishing.

Billings, P. (2019). Regulating crimmigrants through the 'character test': Exploring the consequences of mandatory visa cancellation for the fundamental rights of non-citizens in Australia. *Crime, Law and Social Change, 71*(1), 1–23.

Bjornstrom, E. E. S., Kaufman, R. L., Peterson, R. D., & Slater, M. D. (2010). Race and ethnic representations of law breakers and victims in crime news: A national study of television coverage. *Social Problems, 57*(2), 269–293. https://doi.org/10.1525/sp.2010.57.2.269

Bolt, A. (2011, August 13). Column: Revolt of the ferals. Blog. *The Daily Telegraph*. https://www.dailytelegraph.com.au/blogs/andrew-bolt/column–revolt-of-the-ferals/news-story/1e4efa47f3fa86c79a3c85ace1790898

Bolt, A. (2014, January 26). Why did police and reporters not mention 200 brawling Africans in the middle of Melbourne? Blog. *Herald Sun*. https://www.heraldsun.com.au/blogs/andrew-bolt/why-did-police-and-reporters-not-mention-200-brawling-africans-in-the-middle-of-melbourne/news-story/864c9be518a83b25c227d27dac85c61c

Bolt, A. (2016, March 13). Gangs brawl in Melbourne. Why did we import this danger? Blog. *Herald Sun*. https://www.heraldsun.com.au/blogs/andrew-bolt/gangs-brawl-in-melbourne-why-did-we-import-this-danger/news-story/0bb2ce3addd60e5e8ed849fe7325695e

Bosworth, M., & Guild, M. (2008). Governing through migration control: Security and citizenship in Britain. *British Journal of Criminology*, *48*(6), 703–719.

Bottoms, A. (1995). The politics of sentencing reform. In C. Clarkson & R. Morgan (Eds.), *The philosophy and politics of punishment and sentencing*. Oxford University Press.

Bowling, B., & Phillips, C. (2007). Disproportionate and discriminatory: Reviewing the evidence on police stop and search. *The Modern Law Review*, *70*(6), 936–961.

Bridges, L. (n.d.). The met gangs matrix: Institutional racism in action. *Institute of Race Relations*. https://irr.org.uk/article/the-met-gangs-matrix-institutional-racism-in-action/

Bucci, N. (2018, January 11). 'How long since you've been out for dinner?': Police chief rubbishes 'gang crisis'. *The Age*. https://www.theage.com.au/national/victoria/how-long-since-youve-been-out-for-dinner-police-chief-rubbishes-gang-crisis-20180110-h0gcn9.html

Buttler, M., & Galloway, A. (2016, November 17). Repeat teen offence rates are through the roof as state battles youth crime wave. *Herald Sun*. https://www.heraldsun.com.au/news/law-order/repeat-teen-offence-rates-are-through-roof-as-state-battles-youth-crime-wave/news-story/c01aa9837b3693a2c748492d5c53cdd9

Calligeros, M. (2016, March 13). Violence erupts in Melbourne's CBD as gangs clash in Federation Square and Swanston Street. *The Age*. https://www.theage.com.au/national/victoria/violence-erupts-in-melbournes-cbd-as-gangs-clash-in-federation-square-and-swanston-street-20160313-gnhksv.html

Cassity, E., & Gow, G. (2005). Making up for lost time: The experiences of Southern Sudanese young refugees in high schools. *Youth Studies Australia*, *24*(3), 51.

Chambliss, W. (1999). *Power, politics and crime*. Westview Press.

Chan, J. (1997). *Changing police culture: Policing in a multicultural society*. Cambridge University Press.

Chermak, S. M. (1994). Body count news: How crime is presented in the news media. *Justice Quarterly*, *11*(4), 561–582. https://doi.org/10.1080/07418829400092431

Chibnall, S. (1977). *Law-and-order news: An analysis of crime reporting in the British press*. Tavistock Publications Limited.

Chingaipe, S. (2017, February 25–March 3). Race, stereotyping and Melbourne's Apex gang. *The Saturday Paper*, p. 145.

Chivaura, R. S. (2019). *Blackness as a defining identity: Mediated representations and the lived experiences of African immigrants in Australia*. Springer.

Cohen, S. (1972/2011). *Folk devils and moral panics: The creation of the mods and rockers*. Routledge.

Colic-Peisker, V., & Tilbury, F. (2008). Being black in Australia: A case study of intergroup relations. *Race & Class*, *49*(4), 38–56.

Collins, J., Reid, C., & Fabiansson, C. (2011). Identities, aspirations and belonging of cosmopolitan youth in Australia. *Cosmopolitan Civil Societies: An Interdisciplinary Journal, 3*(3), 92–107.

Connell, K. (2015). *Policing the crisis* 25 years on. *Contemporary British History, 29*(2), 273–283.

Cornwell, B., & Linders, A. (2002). The myth of 'moral panic': An alternative account of LSD prohibition. *Deviant Behavior, 23*(4), 307–330.

Correa-Velez, I., Gifford, S. M., & Barnett, A. G. (2010). Longing to belong: Social inclusion and wellbeing among youth with refugee backgrounds in the first three years in Melbourne, Australia. *Social Science & Medicine, 71*(8), 1399–1408.

Cowie, T. (2016, April 29). Police charge 34, some with links to Apex, over Moomba riots. *The Age.* https://www.theage.com.au/national/victoria/police-charge-34-some-with-links-to-apex-over-moomba-riots-20160429-goht6c.html

Crime Statistics Agency. (2018, January 22). *Correction of country of birth data incorrectly reported and attributed to the Crime Statistics Agency.* Crime Statistics Agency media centre. https://www.crimestatistics.vic.gov.au/media-centre/news/correction-of-country-of-birth-data-incorrectly-reported-and-attributed-to-the

Cunneen, C. (2001). *Conflict, politics and crime.* Allen & Unwin.

Cunneen, C. (2006). Racism, discrimination and the over-representation of indigenous people in the criminal justice system: Some conceptual and explanatory issues. *Current Issues in Criminal Justice, 17*(3), 329–345.

Cunneen, C. (2011). Punishment: Two decades of penal expansionism and its effects on Indigenous imprisonment. *Australian Indigenous Law Review, 15*(1), 8–17.

Cunneen, C. (2020). Youth justice and racialization: Comparative reflections. *Theoretical Criminology, 24*(3), 521–539. https://doi.org/10.1177/1362480619889039

Dandy, J., & Pe-Pua, R. (2010). Attitudes to multiculturalism, immigration and cultural diversity: Comparison of dominant and non-dominant groups in three Australian states. *International Journal of Intercultural Relations, 34*(1), 34–46.

Das Gupta, T., James, C. E., Maaka, R., Galabuzi, G., & Andersen, C. (Eds.). (2007). *Race and racialization: Essential readings.* Canadian Scholars' Press Inc.

Dawes, G., Coventry, G., Moston, S., & Palmer, D. (2014). Sudanese Australians and crime: Police and community perspectives. *Trends and Issues in Crime and Criminal Justice, 477.* https://www.aic.gov.au/publications/tandi/tandi477

Delibasic, S., & Travers, B. (2020, June 19). Streets of hell ahead. *Herald Sun.* Document HERSUN0020200618eg6j0001o.

Deng, S. A. (2017). *Fitting the jigsaw: South Sudanese family dynamics and parenting practices in Australia.* Doctoral dissertation. https://vuir.vu.edu.au/33260/1/DENG %20Santino%20Atem%20-%20thesis.pdf

Department of Premier and Cabinet. (2017). *Victoria's diverse population: 2016 census.* State of Victoria.

Donelly, B. (2014, March 14). Three police officers sacked, others disciplined over racist Sunshine stubby holders. *The Age.* https://www.theage.com.au/national/victoria/three-police-officers-sacked-others-disciplined-over-racist-sunshine-stubby-holders-20140305-346mq.html

Dowsley, A. (2009, September 25). Brawl involving 200 youths erupts at Highpoint Shopping Centre in Melbourne. *Herald Sun.* http://www.heraldsun.com.au/news/brawl-involving-200-youths-erupts-at-highpoint-shopping-centre-in-melbourne/news-story/c26a60c756bc6ebcb775c65de7cc4579?sv=9f21c54506d27d9bb233fff9e91db079

Dubber, M. (2002). *Victims in the war on crime: The use and abuse of victims' rights.* New York University Press.

Due, D. (2008). 'Who are strangers?': Absorbing Sudanese refugees into a white Australia. *ACRAWSA e-journal, 4*(1), 1–13.

Dunn, K. M. (2004). *Racism in Australia: Findings of a survey on racist attitudes and experiences of racism.* Technical paper. https://openresearch-repository.anu.edu.au/handle/1885/41761

Economou, N. (2018, November 26). Victorian state election: Federal antics to blame for Liberals' failure. *Monash Lens.* https://www.google.com/url?q=https://lens.monash.edu/2018/11/26/1365490/federal-antics-to-blame-for-liberals-failure&sa=D&ust=1559796481673000&usg=AFQjCNEe9v4oQ2hXYKsFFHPajbn89Hv4mQ

El-Gack, N., & Yak, G. (2016). A degree doesn't count for South Sudanese job seekers. *The Conversation.* https://theconversation.com/a-degree-doesnt-count-for-south-sudanese-job-seekers-64667

Enrique-Gomes, L. (2018, July 24). Victorian anti-gang laws could target 14-year-olds with no criminal record. *The Guardian.* https://www.theguardian.com/australia-news/2018/jul/24/victorian-anti-gang-laws-condemned-as-guilt-by-association-for-teenagers

Fanon, F. (1986). *Black skin, white masks.* Pluto Press.

Farnsworth, S. (2017, April). Apex crime gang declared a 'non-entity' by Victoria Police. *ABC News.* Document ABCNEW0020170412ed4c000e8.

Farouque, F., Petrie, A., & Miletic, D. (2007, October 2). Minister cuts African refugee intake. *The Age.* https://www.theage.com.au/national/minister-cuts-african-refugee-intake-20071002-ge5yb1.html

Farquharson, K., & Nolan, D. (2018). In a context of crime: Sudanese and South Sudanese Australians in the media. In D. Nolan, K. Farquharson, & T. Marjoribanks (Eds.), *Australian media and the politics of belonging* (pp. 85–104). Anthem Press.

Fatsis, L. (2021). Policing the union's black: The racial politics of law and order in contemporary Britain. In F. Gordon & D. Newman (Eds.), *Leading works in law and social justice.* Routledge.

Ferguson, R. (2018, September). I'm not a gang, not a criminal. *The Australian.* Document AUSTOL0020180926ee9q002mh.

Fernandes, A. (2020, October 20). Mamer came to Australia as a refugee. He committed a violent crime. Can he be deported back to a war-torn country? *SBS News.* https://www.sbs.com.au/news/mamer-came-to-australia-as-a-refugee-he-committed-a-violent-crime-can-he-be-deported-back-to-a-war-torn-country

Fife-Yeomans, J. (2019, June 12). NSW Police target Sudanese crime groups. *The Daily Telegraph.* Document NLDLTW0020190612ef6c004jx.

Fitz-Gibbon, K., Maher, J. M., McCulloch, J., & Segrave, M. (2019). Understanding and responding to family violence risks to children: Evidence-based risk assessment for children and the importance of gender. *Australian and New Zealand Journal of Criminology, 52*(1), 23–40. https://doi.org/10.1177/0004865818760378

Fleury-Steiner, B., Dunn, K., & Fleury-Steiner, R. (2009). Governing through crime as commonsense racism: Race, space, and death penalty 'reform' in Delaware. *Punishment and Society, 11*(1), 5–24.

Florance, L. (2018, January 10). Victoria Police establish African-Australian community taskforce to tackle youth crime. *ABC News.* https://www.abc.net.au/news/2018-01-10/victoria-police-establish-african-australian-community-taskforce/9317898

Forrest, J., & Dunn, K. (2013). Cultural diversity, racialisation and the experience of racism in rural Australia: The South Australian case. *Journal of Rural Studies, 30*, 1–9.

Franko, K. (2020). *The crimmigrant other: Migration and penal power*. Routledge.

Galloway, A., Doherty, E., & Jefferson, A. (2016, March 14). Out of control. *Herald Sun*, p. 5.

Gamlen, A., & Wickes, R. (2018, March 16). Deconstructing 'African gangs'. *Monash Lens*. https://lens.monash.edu/2018/03/15/1332819?slug=unlocking-the-fear-and-myths-around-african-gangs-in-melbourne

Garland, D. (2001). *The culture of control*. Oxford University Press.

Garland, D. (2008). On the concept of moral panic. *Crime, Media, Culture, 4*(1), 9–30.

Gilliam, F. D., Iyengar, S., Simon, A., & Wright, O. (1996). Crime in black and white: The violent, scary world of local news. *Harvard International Journal of Press/Politics, 1*(3), 6–23. https://doi.org/10.1177/1081180X96001003003

Gilroy, P. (1987). *There ain't no black in the Union Jack*. Hutchinson.

Goddard, T., & Myers, R. (2017). Against evidence-based oppression: Marginalized youth and the politics of risk-based assessment and intervention. *Theoretical Criminology, 21*(2), 151–167.

Goldsworthy, T. (2018, November 5). Three charts on: Representation of Australian, New Zealand and Sudan born people in Victorian crime statistics. *The Conversation*. https://theconversation.com/three-charts-on-representation-of-australian-new-zealand-and-sudan-born-people-in-victorian-crime-statistics-101308

Gonzalez Van Cleve, N., & Mayes, L. (2015). Criminal justice through 'colorblind' lenses: A call to examine the mutual constitution of race and criminal justice. *Law & Social Inquiry, 40*(2), 406–432.

Goode, E., & Ben-Yehuda, N. (1994). *Moral panics: The social construction of deviance*. Wiley.

Grabosky, P. N., & Wilson, P. R. (1989). *Journalism and justice: How crime is reported*. Pluto Press.

Green, M. (2015, September 23). Victoria Police officially prohibits racial profiling. *The Age*. https://www.theage.com.au/national/victoria/victoria-police-officially-prohibits-racial-profiling-20150923-gjt6bt.html

Greer, C., & Reiner, R. (2012). Mediated mayhem: Media, crime and criminal justice. In M. Maguire, R. Morgan, & R. Reiner (Eds.), *Oxford handbook of criminology* (pp. 245–278). Oxford University Press.

Grossman, M., & Sharples, J. (2010). *Don't go there: Young people's perspectives on community safety and policing*. Victoria University.

Guy, M., & [@MatthewGuyMP]. (2016a, March 13). When you are fine with 'passive' policing, non pursuit policies and closing stations it ends up with riots at Moomba. Victoria under labor [Tweet]. *Twitter*. https://twitter.com/MatthewGuyMP/status/708921412048674816

Guy, M., & [@MatthewGuyMP] (2016b, March 16). Life under Labor: Crime skyrocketing, police numbers cut and stations closing. Gang violence, random shootings [Tweet]. *Twitter*. https://twitter.com/MatthewGuyMP/status/710229250645688321

Guy, M. (2017a, January 23). Guy: 'One strike and you're out' and presumption of remand for those charged with violence offences. https://electionwatch.unimelb.edu.au/__data/assets/pdf_file/0008/2930453/Coal-One-Strike-Bail.pdf

Guy, M. (2017b, March 28). Matthew Guy: Time to tackle crime and make Victoria safe again. *Herald Sun*. http://www.heraldsun.com.au/news/opinion/matthew-guy-time-to-tackle-crime-and-make-victoria-safe-again/news-story/15df15b68f69991ef4 e26501b9730148

Guy, M. [@MatthewGuyMP]. (2018, January 2). The Police Minister admits – In the middle of a law and order and African gang crisis – That she has no idea who is in charge of the state as Andrews, Merlino and Allen are all MIA [Tweet]. *Twitter*. https://twitter.com/MatthewGuyMP/status/948170970853916672

Haggerty, K. D., & Ericson, R. V. (2000). The surveillant assemblage. *British Journal of Sociology*, *51*(4), 605–622.

Haile-Michael, D., & Issa, M. (2015). *The more things change, the more they stay the same: Report of the FKCLC Peer Advocacy Outreach Project on racial profiling across Melbourne*. Flemington and Kensington Community Legal Centre. http://www.policeaccountability.org.au/wp-content/uploads/2015/07/More-Things-Change_report_softcopy.pdf

Hall, S. (1979). *Drifting into a law and order society*. Cobden Trust.

Hall, S., Critcher, C., Jefferson, T., Clarke, J., & Roberts, B. (1978). *Policing the crisis: Mugging, the state, and law and order*. MacMillan.

Hallsworth, S., & Young, T. (2008). Gang talk and gang talkers: A critique. *Crime, Media, Culture*, *4*(2), 175–195. https://doi.org/10.1177/1741659008092327

Hamblin, A., & Cavanagh, R. (2016, March 8). Teen detainees end roof standoff with police at Melbourne Youth Justice Centre. *Herald Sun*. https://www.heraldsun.com.au/news/victoria/teen-detainees-in-roof-standoff-at-melbourne-youth-justice-centre/news-story/397794d10a0bcd22493eb7fa3a04a2ab

Harcourt, B. (2015). Risk as a proxy for race: The dangers of risk assessment. *Federal Sentencing Reporter*, *27*(4), 237–243.

Hatoss, A. (2012). Where are you from? Identity construction and experiences of 'othering' in the narratives of Sudanese refugee-background Australians. *Discourse & Society*, *23*(1), 47–68.

Hawkins, D. H. (Ed.). (1995). *Ethnicity, race, and crime: Perspectives across time and place*. State University Press of New York.

Hebbani, A., Obijiofor, L., & Bristed, H. (2009). Generational differences faced by Sudanese refugee women settling in Australia. *Intercultural Communication Studies*, *18*(1), 66.

Henriques-Gomes, L. (2018). South Sudanese-Australians report racial abuse intensified after 'African gangs' claims. *The Guardian*, p. 4.

Herald Sun. (2019, December 30). Opinion piece. Document HERSUN002019 1229efcu000obj.

Hervik, P. (Ed.). (2019). *Racialization, racism and anti-racism in the Nordic countries*. Palgrave.

Hier, S. (2008). Thinking beyond moral panic: Risk, responsibility and the politics of moralization. *Theoretical Criminology*, *12*(2), 173–190.

Hogg, R., & Brown, D. (1998). *Rethinking law and order*. Pluto Press.

Hopkins, N. (2011). Dual identities and their recognition: Minority group members' perspectives. *Political Psychology*, *32*(2), 251–270.

Horsley, M. (2017). Forget moral panics. *Journal of Theoretical and Philosophical Criminology*, *9*(2), 84–98.

Horton, J. (1979). Review of policing the crisis. *Crime and Social Justice, 12*(Winter), 59–63.

Hosking, W. (2016, May 19). Victoria Police and Herald Sun join forces on youth crime scourge. *Herald Sun.*

Houston, T., Mills, A., & Dow, C. (2016, March 15). Police ignored warnings about planned rampage – City rampage – Moomba organisers told of possible gang arrivals. *The Age,* p. 4.

IPSOS. (2015). The top issues facing Australia September 2015. https://www.ipsos.com/sites/default/files/2017-07/Ipsos-Issues-Monitor-July-to-September-2015-National-Victoria.pdf

IPSOS. (2016). IPSOS issues monitor March 2016. https://www.ipsos.com/sites/default/files/2017-07/IM_AUS_VIC_Mar16.pdf

IPSOS. (2018). IPSOS issues monitor December 2018: The top issues facing Australia. https://www.ipsos.com/sites/default/files/ct/news/documents/2019-01/im_vic_dec18_v1.pdf

Jayasuriya, L. (2003). *Legacies of white Australia: Race, culture, and nation.* University of Western Australia Press.

Joint Standing Committee on Migration. (2017). *No one teaches you to become an Australian.* Parliament of the Commonwealth of Australia. https://parlinfo.aph.gov.au/parlInfo/download/committees/reportjnt/024098/toc_pdf/NooneteachesyoutobecomeanAustralian.pdf;fileType=application%2Fpdf

Jones, R. (2021). It's the best job on the paper: The courts beat during the journalism crisis. *Journalism Practice,* 1–22. https://doi.org/10.1080/17512786.2021.1910980

Kamaloni, S. (2019). *Understanding racism in a post-racial world visible invisibilities.* Palgrave Macmillan.

Kehl, D., Guo, P., & Kessler, S. (2017). *Algorithms in the criminal justice system: Assessing the use of risk assessments in sentencing.* Responsive Communities Initiative, Berkman Klein Centre for Internet & Society, Harvard Law School.

Keith, M. (Ed.). (1993). Discipline? In *Racism, the city and the state* (p. 193). Routledge.

Kelly, A. (2015, January 13). The pointy end of police racism: A Ken Lay retrospective. *New Matilda.* https://newmatilda.com/2015/01/13/pointy-end-police-racism-ken-lay-retrospective/

Kenny, C. (2018, January 3). 'Frankly they don't belong in Australian society': Dutton comes down hard on Sudanese crime gangs. *2GB.* https://www.2gb.com/frankly-they-dont-belong-in-australian-society-dutton-comes-down-hard-on-sudanese-crime-gangs/

Khan, S., & Pedersen, A. (2010). Black African immigrants to Australia: Prejudice and the function of attitudes. *Journal of Pacific Rim Psychology, 4*(2), 116–129.

Kingdon, J. (1984). *Agenda, alternatives, and public policies.* Little, Brown.

Klein, R. D., & Naccarato, S. (2003). Broadcast news portrayal of minorities: Accuracy in reporting. *American Behavioral Scientist, 46*(12), 1611–1616. https://doi.org/10.1177/0002764203254617

Koulish, R., & van der Woude, M. (2020). *Crimmigrant nations: Resurgent nationalism and the closing of borders.* Fordham University Press.

Koumouris, G., & Blaustein, J. (2021). Reporting 'African gangs': Theorising journalistic practice during a multi-mediated moral panic. *Crime, Media, Culture.* https://doi.org/10.1177/1741659021991205

Koziol, M. (2017, April). Apex gang defunct as leaders jailed. *The Age*. Document AGEE000020170412ed4d00013.

Lacey, N. (2008). *The prisoners' dilemma*. Cambridge University Press.

Lambert, N. M., Stillman, T. F., Hicks, J. A., Kamble, S., Baumeister, R. F., & Fincham, F. D. (2013). To belong is to matter: Sense of belonging enhances meaning in life. *Personality and Social Psychology Bulletin, 39*(11), 1418–1427.

Lane, B. (2018, November). African crime story. *The Australian*. Document AUSTOL0020181119eebj003xq.

Law Institute of Victoria. (2017, July 7). A joint open letter to the Attorney-General and Ministers Mikakos and Neville on youth justice reform. https://www.liv. asn.au/Staying-Informed/General-News/General-News/June-2017/A-joint-open-letter-to-the-Attorney-General-and-Mi

Lianos, M. (Ed.). (2013). Normative otherness: From 'sovereign subjects' to 'collateral damage'. In *Dangerous others, insecure societies: Fear and social division* (pp. 69–86). Ashgate.

Lianos, M., & Douglas, M. (2000). Dangerization and the end of deviance: The institutional environment. *The British Journal of Criminology, 40*(2), 261–278.

Linden, A. (2015). Conducting interrupted time-series analysis for single- and multiple-group comparisons. *The Stata Journal, 15*(2), 480–500. https://doi.org/10.1177/1536867X1501500208

Loader, I. (2006). Policing, recognition and belonging. *Annals of the American Academy of Political and Social Science, 605*, 201–221.

Long, L. (2018). *Perpetual suspects: A critical race theory of black and mixed-race experiences of policing*. Palgrave Macmillan.

Longazel, J. G. (2013). Moral panic as racial degradation ceremony: Racial stratification and the local-level backlash against Latino/a immigrants. *Punishment & Society, 15*(1), 96–119.

Longshore, D., Chang, E., & Messina, N. (2005). Self-control and social bonds: A combined control perspective on juvenile offending. *Journal of Quantitative Criminology, 21*(4), 419–437.

Losoncz, I. (2011). Blocked opportunity and threatened identity: Understanding experiences of disrespect in South Sudanese Australians. *Australasian Review of African Studies, 32*(2), 118.

Losoncz, I. (2017). Goals without means: A Mertonian critique of Australia's resettlement policy for South Sudanese refugees. *Journal of Refugee Studies, 30*(1), 47–70.

Macaulay, L., & Deppeler, J. (2020). Perspectives on negative media representations of Sudanese and South Sudanese youths in Australia. *Journal of Intercultural Studies, 41*(2), 213–230.

MacDonald, F. (2017). Positioning young refugees in Australia: Media discourse and social exclusion. *International Journal of Inclusive Education, 21*(11), 1182–1195.

Macek, S. (2006). *Urban nightmares: The media, the right, and the moral panic over the city*. University of Minnesota Press.

Maher, S. L. (2018). *The post-settlement lives of South Sudanese Australian women: Surviving and belonging*. Monash University.

Maher, S., Blaustein, J., Benier, K., Chitambo, J., & Johns, D. (2020). Mothering after Moomba: Labelling, secondary stigma and maternal efficacy in the post-settlement context. *Theoretical Criminology*. https://doi.org/10.1177/1362480620981639

Maher, S., Deng, S., & Kindersley, N. (2018). South Sudanese Australians: Constantly negotiating belonging and identity. *Sudan Studies, 58*, 53–65.

Majavu, M. (2017). *Uncommodified blackness: The African male experience in Australia and New Zealand.* Springer.

Majavu, M. (2018). The whiteness regimes of multiculturalism: The African male experience in Australia. *Journal of Asian and African Studies, 53*(2), 187–200.

Majavu, M. (2020). The 'African gangs' narrative: Associating blackness with criminality and other anti-black racist tropes in Australia. *African and Black Diaspora: An International Journal, 13*(1), 27–39.

Mapedzahama, V., & Kwansah-Aidoo, K. (2013). Negotiating diasporic black African existence in Australia: A reflective analysis. *Australasian Review of African Studies, 34*(1), 61–81.

Mapedzahama, V., & Kwansah-Aidoo, K. (2017). Blackness as burden? The lived experience of black Africans in Australia. *Sage Open, 7*(3). 2158244017720483.

Marion, N. (1997). Symbolic policies in Clinton's crime control agenda. *Buffalo Criminal Law Review, 1*(1), 67–108.

Markus, A. (2015). *Mapping social cohesion: The Scanlon foundation surveys 2015.* Monash University. https://scanlonfoundation.org.au/wp-content/uploads/2018/10/2015-Mapping-Social-Cohesion-Report.pdf

Markus, A. B. (2016). Australians today: The Australia@2015 Scanlon foundation survey. Australian Centre for Jewish Civilisation, Monash University.

Markus, A. B., Jupp, J., & McDonald, P. (2009). *Australia's immigration revolution.* Allen & Unwin.

Martin, P. (2018, January 13). The gang crisis our leaders help create. *The Sydney Morning Herald.* https://www.smh.com.au/opinion/the-gang-crime-our-leaders-help-create-20180112-h0hgvf.html

Massey, D. S. (2015). A missing element in migration theories. *Migration Letters, 12*(3), 279–299.

Mayek, M. (2018, January 12). It's time for our voices to be heard beyond the #Africangangs campaign. *The Guardian.* https://www.theguardian.com/commentisfree/2018/jan/12/its-time-for-our-voice-to-be-heard-beyond-the-africangangs-campaign

McAdam, J. (2013). The problem of 'crisis migration'. *Australian Journal of Human Rights, 19*(3), 7–28.

McCulloch, J., & Wilson, D. (2016). *Pre-crime: Pre-emption, precaution and the future.* Routledge.

McMullan, J. L., & Ratner, R. S. (1982). Review of policing the crisis. *The Canadian Journal of Sociology, 7*(2), 231–239.

McPherson, W. (1999, February). *The Stephen Lawrence inquiry.* London: Stationery Office. https://assets.publishing.service.gov.uk/government/uploads/system/uploads/attachment_data/file/277111/4262.pdf

McRobbie, A., & Thornton, S. L. (1995). Rethinking 'moral panic' for multi-mediated social worlds. *The British Journal of Sociology, 46*(4), 559–574.

Mickelburough, P. (2011, August 22). Victoria Police monitoring gangs in Melbourne following British riots. *Herald Sun.* https://amp.heraldsun.com.au/ipad/victoria-police-monitoring-gangs-in-melbourne-following-british-riots/news-story/55aba93da2a1ddbc5b1ed4ce65bbdf78

Miller, L. (2008). *The perils of federalism: Race, poverty, and the politics of crime control*. Oxford University Press.

Mills, T., & Hall, B. (2017, January 7) Apex fears spark concerns about racial profiling. *The Age*. https://www.theage.com.au/national/victoria/apex-fears-spark-concerns-about-racial-profiling-20161123-gsvete.html

Mills, T., & Houston, C. (2016, March 14). Melbourne CBD brawl: Who are the Apex gang? *The Age*. https://www.theage.com.au/national/victoria/melbourne-cbd-brawl-who-are-the-apex-gang-20160314-gnima2.html

Millsteed, M., & Sutherland, P. (2016). How has youth crime in Victoria changed over the past 10 years? *In fact, no. 3*. Crime Statistics Agency, Victoria.

Morton, R. (2016, July). Kids are growing with very little structure. *The Australian*. Document AUSTLN0020160725ec7q0003a.

Murji, K. (2006). Racialization. In E. McLaughlin & J. Muncie (Eds.), *The Sage dictionary of criminology* (pp. 334–335). Sage.

Murji, K. (2020). Stuart Hall as a criminological theorist-activist. *Theoretical Criminology*, *24*(3), 447–460.

Murray, D. (2018, March). Yet even harder to discuss than speed of migration is the identity of migrants. *The Australian*. Document AUSTOL0020180317ee3g00001.

Ndhlovu, F. (2013). 'Too tall, too dark' to be Australian: Racial perceptions of post-refugee Africans. *Critical Race & Whiteness Studies*, *9*(2), 1–17.

Ndhlovu, F. (2014). *Becoming an African diaspora in Australia: Language, culture, identity*. Palgrave Macmillan.

Neville, L. (2018, September 20). Crime continues to fall. Premier of Victoria. https://www.premier.vic.gov.au/crime-continues-to-fall/

Newburn, T. (2007). 'Tough on crime': Penal policy in England and Wales. *Crime and Justice*, *36*(1), 425–470.

Newburn, T. (2015). The 2011 England riots in recent historical perspective. *British Journal of Criminology*, *55*(1), 39–64.

Newburn, T., & Jones, T. (2005). Symbolic politics and penal populism: The long shadow of Willie Horton. *Crime, Media, Culture: International Journal*, *1*(1), 72–87.

Newburn, T., Jones, T., & Blaustein, J. (2018). Framing the 2011 England riots: Understanding the political and policy response. *The Howard Journal of Crime and Justice*, *57*(3), 339–362.

Noble, G. (2005). The discomfort of strangers: Racism, incivility and ontological security in a relaxed and comfortable nation. *Journal of Intercultural Studies*, *26*(1–2), 107–120.

Nolan, D., Farquharson, K., & Marjoribanks, T. (Eds.). (2018). *Australian media and the politics of belonging*. Anthem Press.

Nolan, D., Farquharson, K., Marjoribanks, T., & Muller, D. (2014). *The AuSud media project 2011–2013 final report*. University of Melbourne. https://arts.unimelb.edu.au/__data/assets/pdf_file/0006/1760163/Report_AuSud_Media_Project2014.pdf

Nutt, T. (2019). *2018 Victorian state election review. Report to the administrative committee*. Liberal Party, Victoria.

Nyuon, N. (2018, November 24–30). The Victorian election and the politics of fear. *The Saturday Paper*, p. 232.

O'Donohue, E. (2016, March 14). Today, Daniel Andrews...? *[Facebook]*. https://www.facebook.com/ODonohueMLC/posts/1713448902235974

O'Malley, P. (1994). Neo-liberal crime control: Political agendas and the future of crime prevention in Australia. In D. Chappell & P. Wilson (Eds.), *The Australian criminal justice system. The mid 1990s* (4th ed.). Butterworths.

O'Malley, P. (2000). Criminologies of catastrophe? Understanding criminal justice on the edge of the new millennium. *Australian and New Zealand Journal of Criminology, 33*(2), 153–167.

O'Malley, P. (2010). Simulated justice: Risk, money and telemetric policing. *British Journal of Criminology, 50*(5), 795–807.

Oriel, J. (2018, January). One would have thought a mob of African males invading. *The Australian.* Document AUSTOL0020180107ee17000xe.

Page, J. (2011). *The toughest beat: Politics, punishment and the prison officers union in California.* Oxford University Press.

Palmer, D., Frederick, G., & Coventry, A. (2020). *Crime, criminalization and refugees: The case of Sudanese Australians.* Springer-Verlag.

Parmar, A. (2017). Policing belonging. In M. Bosworth, A. Parmar, & Y. Vazquez (Eds.), *Race, criminal justice and migration control: Enforcing the boundaries of belonging* (pp. 108–124). Oxford University Press.

Parmar, A., Earle, R., Parmar, A., & Phillips, C. (2020). Race matters in criminology: Introduction to the special issue. *Theoretical Criminology, 24*(3), 421–426.

Pearlman, J. (2007, October 5). Andrews, Howard deny racism. *Sydney Morning Herald.* https://www.smh.com.au/national/andrews-howard-deny-racism-20071005-gdr9o2.html

Pettigrew, T. F., & Tropp, L. R. (2006). A meta-analytic test of intergroup contact theory. *Journal of Personality and Social Psychology, 90*(5), 751.

Phillips, C., & Bowling, B. (2017). Ethnicities, racism, crime, and criminal justice. In A. Liebling, S. Maruna, & L. McAra (Eds.), *The Oxford handbook of criminology.* Oxford University Press.

Police Accountability Project. (n.d.). Equality is not the same: The next steps. https://www.policeaccountability.org.au/issues-and-cases/racial-profiling/victoria-police-inquiry/

Powell, R., & Martin, D. (2018). Submission to Legal and Constitutional Affairs Legislation Committee on the Migration Amendment (Strengthening the Character Test) Bill 2018. https://www.monash.edu/__data/assets/pdf_file/0005/1731992/Border-Crossing-Observatory_Submission_Migration-Amendment-Strengthening-the-Character-Test-Bill-2018_3Dec2018.pdf

Pratt, J. (1998). *Governing the dangerous: Dangerousness, law, and social change.* Federation Press.

Pratt, J. (2017). Risk control, rights and legitimacy in the limited liability state. *British Journal of Criminology, 57*(6), 1322–1339.

Pratt, J., Brown, D., Brown, M., Hallsworth, S., & Morrison, J. (Eds.). (2005). *The new punitiveness: Trends, theories, perspectives.* Willan Publishing.

Pritchard, D., & Hughes, K. D. (1997). Patterns of deviance in crime news. *Journal of Communication, 47*(3), 49–67.

Refugee Council. (2018). Key facts on the conflict in South Sudan. https://www.refugeecouncil.org.au/south-sudan/#:~:text=Around%2024%2C000%20South%20Sudanese%20people,refugees%20had%20settled%20into%20Australia

Refugee Health Research Centre. (2007). Promoting partnerships with police (broadsheet #2). Refugee Health Research Centre.

Reiner, R. (1978). Review of policing the crisis. *The British Journal of Sociology*, *29*(4), 511–512. Special Issue: Contemporary Britain: Aspects and Approaches.

Renzaho, A. M., Green, J., Mellor, D., & Swinburn, B. (2011). Parenting, family functioning and lifestyle in a new culture: The case of African migrants in Melbourne, Victoria, Australia. *Child & Family Social Work*, *16*(2), 228–240.

Robinson, J. (2013). People of Sudanese heritage living in Australia: Implications of demography for individual and community resilience. In J. Marlowe, A. Harris, & T. Lyons (Eds.), *South Sudanese diaspora in Australia and New Zealand: Reconciling the past with the present* (pp. 12–47). Cambridge Scholars Publishing.

Rood, D. (2010, November 8). Victoria decides: The key issues – Law and order. *The Age*. https://www.theage.com.au/national/victoria/victoria-decides-the-key-issues-20101107-17izg.html

Rose, N. (1999). *Powers of freedom: Reframing political thought*. Cambridge University Press.

Run, P. (2013). Unnecessary encounters: South Sudanese refugees' experiences of racial profiling in Melbourne. *Social Alternatives*, *32*(3), 20–25.

Ryan, J. P., Testa, M. F., & Zhai, F. (2008). African American males in foster care and the risk of delinquency: The value of social bonds and permanence. *Child Welfare*, *87*(1), 115–140.

Sampson, R., & Gifford, S. M. (2010). Place-making, settlement and well-being: The therapeutic landscapes of recently arrived youth with refugee backgrounds. *Health & Place*, *16*(1), 116–131.

Sampson, R. J., & Laub, J. H. (1990). Crime and deviance over the life course: The salience of adult social bonds. *American Sociological Review*, *55*(5), 609–627.

SBS News. (2016, November 4). Dozens charged after Melbourne CBD riot. *SBS News*. https://www.sbs.com.au/news/dozens-charged-after-melbourne-cbd-riot

SBS News. (2018). Victoria Police, African community join forces for youth crime taskforce. https://www.sbs.com.au/news/victoria-police-african-community-join-forces-for-youth-crime-taskforce

Schlesinger, P. (1979). Review of policing the crisis. *Sociology*, *13*(2), 323–325.

Schwartz, S. J., Montgomery, M. J., & Briones, E. (2006). The role of identity in acculturation among immigrant people: Theoretical propositions, empirical questions, and applied recommendations. *Human Development*, *49*(1), 1–30.

Seccombe, M. (2019, December 7–13). Algorithms and prejudice. *The Saturday Paper*. https://www.thesaturdaypaper.com.au/news/politics/2019/12/07/algorithms-and-prejudice/15756372009195?cb=1600402923

Sentas, V. (2017, November 2). Pre-emptive policing is harmful and oppressive, and requires independent scrutiny. *The Conversation*. https://theconversation.com/pre-emptive-policing-is-harmful-and-oppressive-and-requires-independent-scrutiny-86206

Sentas, V., & Pandolfini, C. (2017). *Policing young people in NSW: A study of the Suspect Targeting Management Plan – A report of the Youth Justice Coalition NSW*. Youth Justice Coalition NSW. https://www.piac.asn.au/wp-content/uploads/2017/10/17.10.25-YJC-STMP-Report.pdf

Sentencing Advisory Council. (2021). Sentencing outcomes in the Children's Court. https://www.sentencingcouncil.vic.gov.au/statistics/sentencing-trends/sentencing-outcomes-childrens-court

Simon, J. (2002). Governing through crime metaphors. *Brooklyn Law Review*, *67*(4), 1035–1070.

Simon, J. (2007). *Governing through crime: How the war on crime transformed American democracy and created a culture of fear*. Oxford University Press.

Simonis, A., Travers, B., Delibasic, S., & Fagan, J. (2020a, June 17). Melbourne Storm's powerful messages after Solo's death. *Herald Sun*. Document NLHRSW0020 200618eg6h0025t.

Simonis, A., Travers, B., Delibasic, S., & Fagan, J. (2020b, June 17). Police hunt more offenders in schoolboy's death as gang tensions rise. *Herald Sun*. Document NLHRSW0020200617eg6h003s6.

Simonsen, K. (2016). How the host nation's boundary drawing affects immigrants' belonging. *Journal of Ethnic and Migration Studies*, *42*, 1153–1176.

Skolnick, J. (1966). *Justice without trial: Law enforcement in democratic society*. John Wiley & Sons.

Skolnick, J. H. (2007). Racial profiling – Then and now. *Criminology & Public Policy*, *6*(1), 65–70.

Sky News Australia. (2017, December 28). *John Pesutto: Community engagement is important, but so is proper punishment*. https://www.skynews.com.au/australia-news/full-interview-john-pesutto-community-engagement-is-important-but-so-is-proper-punishment/video/ac2137b52bb4ace51497aaf0420ad03b

Smethurst, A., & Buttler, M. (2017, November 19). Sudanese youth crime surges. *Herald Sun*, p. 3.

Smith, R. (2019, January 9). Blood drill killers 'Australia's problem'. *News.com.au*. Document NLNEWW0020190109ef19003ea.

Smith, B., & Reside, S. (2010). Boys, you wanna give me some action?: Interventions in the policing of racialized communities in Melbourne – A report of the 2009/10 racism project. Legal Services Board. http://smls.org.au/wp-content/uploads/2016/09/Boys-Wanna-Give-Me-Some-Action.pdf

Spaaij, R. (2015). Refugee youth, belonging and community sport. *Leisure Studies*, *34*(3), 303–318.

Stark, J. (2014, January 25). African youths in new year's brawl. *The Age*. http://www.theage.com.au/victoria/african-youths-in-new-years-brawl-20140125-31fv6.html

Stevenson, M. (2009). Sudanese migration in Australia. Museums Victoria Collections. https://collections.museumsvictoria.com.au/articles/2997

Strangio, P. (2018, November 25). Victorian labor's thumping win reveals how out of step with voters liberals have become. *The Conversation*. https://theconversation.com/victorian-labors-thumping-win-reveals-how-out-of-step-with-voters-liberals-have-become-105574

Sydes, M., & Wickes, R. (2021). The land of the 'fair go'? Mapping income inequality and socioeconomic segregation across Melbourne neighbourhoods. In *Urban socio-economic segregation and income inequality* (p. 229). Monash University.

Taylor, I. (1999). *Crime in context: A critical criminology of market societies*. Wiley.

Taylor, J. (2004). Refugees and social exclusion: What the literature says. *Migration Action*, *26*(2), 16–31.

Tazreiter, C. (2018). Narratives of crisis migration and the power of visual culture. In C. Menjívar, M. Ruiz, & I. Ness (Eds.), *The Oxford handbook of migration crises*. Oxford University Press.

The Australian. (2018, December 31). Melbourne's African gangs. https://www.theaustralian.com.au/commentary/editorials/melbournes-african-gangs/news-story/e0afb0f7a5bd8fd7c332544dcadaf861

The Economist. (2016). The world's most liveable cities. http://www.economist.com/blogs/graphicdetail/2016/08/daily-chart-14

Thompson, A. (2017, January 1). Apex youth planned crimes from behind bars. *Herald Sun.* https://www.heraldsun.com.au/news/law-order/apex-youth-planned-crimes-from-behind-bars/news-story/6c035311f487c08e37b162d4241f8e3b

Thompson, K., Thompson, K. W., & Kennet, T. (1998). *Moral panics.* Psychology Press.

Tomazin, F. (2018, January 6). Teen gang deportation plan a 'death sentence', Sudanese leaders warn. *The Age.* https://www.theage.com.au/national/victoria/teen-gang-deportation-plan-a-death-sentence-sudanese-leaders-warn-20180106-h0efa8.html

Tonry, M. (2004). *Punishment and politics: Evidence and emulation in the making of English crime control policy.* Routledge.

Travers, B. (2017, January 8). Teenagers riot again at Parkville. *Herald Sun.* https://www.heraldsun.com.au/news/victoria/teenagers-riot-again-at-parkville/news-story/4a510156c1194eb03f4e36e0fae02fcf

Travers, B., & Hosking, W. (2017, February 19). Mayhem as police swarm White Night. *Herald Sun.* https://www.heraldsun.com.au/news/law-order/mayhem-as-police-swarm-white-night/news-story/4a178a81f787cd99916b6bba709792da?utm_content=SocialFlow&utm_campaign=EditorialSF&utm_source=HeraldSun&utm_medium=Twitter

Travers, M. (2005). Evaluation research and criminal justice: Beyond a political critique. *Australian and New Zealand Journal of Criminology, 38*(1), 39–58.

Turk, A. T. (1980). Review of policing the crisis. *American Journal of Sociology, 86*(1), 213–214.

Tyler, T. R. (1997). The psychology of legitimacy: A relational perspective on voluntary deference to authorities. *Personality and Social Psychology Review, 1,* 323–345.

Udah, H. (2018). 'Not by default accepted': The African experience of othering and being othered in Australia. *Journal of Asian and African Studies, 53*(3), 384–400.

Udah, H., & Singh, P. (2019). Identity, othering and belonging: Toward an understanding of difference and the experiences of African immigrants to Australia. *Social Identities, 25*(6), 843–859.

Ugwudike, P. (2020). Digital prediction technologies in the justice system: The implications of a 'race neutral' agenda. *Theoretical Criminology, 24*(3), 482–501.

Vamvakinou, M., & Neumann, S. (2018). *Dissenting report: Labor members.* Parliament of the Commonwealth of Australia. https://www.aph.gov.au/Parliamentary_Business/Committees/Joint/Migration/settlementoutcomes/Report/section?id=committees%2freportjnt%2f024098%2f25527

Vertovec, S. (2017). Mooring, migration milieus and complex explanations. *Ethnic and Racial Studies, 40*(9), 1574–1581. https://doi.org/10.1080/01419870.2017.1308534

Victoria Police. (2013). *Report: 'Equality is not the same…'.* http://www.policeaccountability.org.au/wp-content/uploads/2014/03/Equality-is-not-the-same_Victoria-Police-Response-to-Community-Consultation-and-Reviews1.pdf

Victoria Police. (2016, August 1). Press conference … regarding the Victorian-first Community Safety Statement. *Facebook.* https://www.facebook.com/victoriapolice/videos/press-conference-with-premier-daniel-andrews-minister-for-police-lisa-neville-po/1310268829045250/

Victoria Police. (2018, January 2). *Live media conference*. https://www.facebook.com/victoriapolice/videos/1822198964518898/

Victoria Police. (2021). *Receipting proof of concept*. Programs and initiatives. https://www.police.vic.gov.au/receipting-proof-concept

Victorian Government. (2012). *Review of Victoria Police use of 'stop and search' powers*. https://www.parliament.vic.gov.au/file_uploads/VPARL2010-14No128_bJxK7r5D.pdf

Victorian Ombudsman. (2017). *Report on youth justice facilities at the Grevillea unit of Barwon Prison, Malmsbury and Parkville*. Victorian Ombudsman.

Visentin, L. (2018, December 2). 'My own son cannot get a job now': Sydney's Sudanese hit by Melbourne 'ripple effect'. *The Age*. Document AGEEOL002018 1203eec20008d.

Wacquant, L. (1999). 'Suitable enemies': Foreigners and immigrants in the prisons of Europe. *Punishment & Society, 1*(2), 215–222.

Wacquant, L. (2001a). The penalisation of poverty and the rise of neo-liberalism. *European Journal on Criminal Policy and Research, 9*, 401–412.

Wacquant, L. (2001b). Deadly symbiosis: When ghetto and prison meet and mesh. *Punishment & Society, 3*(1), 95–134.

Wacquant, L. (2002). From slavery to mass incarceration: Rethinking the 'race question' in the US. *New Left Review, 13*, 41–60.

Wacquant, L. (2009). *Punishing the poor: The neoliberal government of social insecurity*. Duke University Press.

Waddington, P. A. J. (1999). *Policing citizens: Authority and rights*. Routledge.

Wahlquist, C. (2018a, January 10). #AfricanGangs: Social media responds to Melbourne's 'crisis'. *The Guardian*. (Australia). https://www.theguardian.com/media/2018/jan/10/africangangs-social-media-responds-to-melbournes-crisis

Wahlquist, C. (2018b, January 11). Daniel Andrews accuses Dutton of trying to 'get rise out of people' over gang comments. *The Guardian*. (Australia). https://www.theguardian.com/australia-news/2018/jan/11/daniel-andrews-accuses-dutton-of-trying-to-get-rise-out-of-people-over-gang-comments

Wahlquist, C. (2018c, January 3). Is Melbourne in the grip of African crime gangs? The facts behind the lurid headlines. *The Guardian*. https://www.theguardian.com/australia-news/2018/jan/03/is-melbourne-in-the-grip-of-african-gangs-the-facts-behind-the-lurid-headlines

Wahlquist, C. (2018d, March 19). Reporting on 'African gangs' akin to 'media terrorism', says Melbourne campaigner. *The Guardian*. https://www.theguardian.com/australia-news/2018/mar/19/reporting-on-african-gangs-akin-to-media-terrorism-says-melbourne-campaigner

Weatherburn, D. (2004). *Law and order in Australia: Rhetoric and reality*. The Federation Press.

Weber, L. (2018, December). *'Police are good for some people, but not for us': Community perspectives on young people, policing and belonging in Greater Dandenong and Casey*. Border Crossing Observatory. https://arts.monash.edu/__data/assets/pdf_file/0004/1621732/Police-are-good-for-some-people,-but-not-for-us.pdf

Weber, L. (2020a, April). 'You're going to be in the system forever': Policing, risk and belonging in Greater Dandenong and Casey. Border Crossing Observatory. https://www.monash.edu/__data/assets/pdf_file/0011/2175959/Youre-going-to-be-in-the-system-forever-June.pdf

Weber, L. (2020b). 'My kids won't grow up here': Policing, bordering and belonging. *Theoretical Criminology*, *24*(1), 71–89. Special issue on policing, migration and national identity.

Weber, L., & Powell, R. (2020). Crime, pre-crime and sub-crime: Deportation of 'risky non-citizens' as 'enemy crimmigration'. In J. Pratt & J. Anderson (Eds.), *Criminal justice, risk and the revolt against uncertainty* (pp. 245–272). Palgrave Macmillan.

Welch, K. (2007). Black criminal stereotypes and racial profiling. *Journal of Contemporary Criminal Justice*, *23*(3), 276–288. https://doi.org/10.1177/104398620 7306870

Welch, M., Price, E., & Yankey, N. (2004). Youth violence and race in the media: The emergence of 'wilding' as an invention of the press. *Race, Gender & Class*, *11*(2), 36–58.

Wickes, R., Grossman, M., Forbes-Mewett, H., Arunachalam, D., Smith, J., Skrbis, Z., Dellal, H., & Keel, C. (2020). *Understanding the context of racial and cultural exclusivism: A study of Melbourne neighbourhoods*. Monash University. https://doi.org/10.26180/5e6ee32b45cdd

Wickramaarachchi, N., & Burns, E. (2016). Sudanese humanitarian migrants in Australian refereed journals. *Australasian Review of African Studies*, *37*(2), 80–106.

Williams, P. (2015). Criminalising the other: Challenging the race-gang nexus. *Race & Class*, *56*(3), 18–35. https://doi.org/10.1177/0306396814556221

Williams, P., & Clarke, B. (2016). *Dangerous associations: Joint enterprise, gangs and racism – An analysis of the processes of criminalisation of black, Asian and minority ethnic individuals*. Centre for Crime and Justice Studies.

Williams, P., & Kind, E. (2019). *Data driven policing: The hardwiring of discriminatory policing practices across Europe*. European Network Against Racism/Open Society.

Willingham, R. (2019, March 29). 'Greens' disastrous 2018 poll blamed on scandals, internal disputes, 'cashed-up' labor. *ABC News*. https://www.abc.net.au/news/2019-03-29/greens-blame-internal-problems-negative-media-for-election-loss/10950124

Willingham, R., & Preiss, B. (2016, March 14). Daniel Andrews warns gangs: 'We are coming after you and you will feel the full force of the law'. *The Age*. https://www.theage.com.au/national/victoria/daniel-andrews-warns-gangs-we-are-coming-after-you-and-you-will-feel-the-full-force-of-the-law-20160314-gnialt.html

Windle, J. (2008). The racialisation of African youth in Australia. *Social Identities: Journal for the Study of Religion, Nature and Culture*, *14*(5), 553–566.

Wonders, N., & Cerys, L. (forthcoming). Challenging the borders of difference and inequality: Power in migration as a social movement for global justice. In L. Weber & C. Tazreiter (Eds.), *Handbook of migration and global justice*. Edward Elgar.

Wood, M. (2017, January 13). For gangs with a social media presence like Apex, there's no such thing as bad publicity. *The Conversation*. http://theconversation.com/for-gangs-with-a-social-media-presence-like-apex-theres-no-such-thing-as-bad-publicity-70730

Woods, E. (2017a, May 12). The young Moomba rioters: Restoring faith in justice. *The Age*. https://www.theage.com.au/national/victoria/the-young-moomba-rioters-restoring-faith-in-justice-20170510-gw1zs0.html

Woods, E. (2017b, May 14). The young Moomba rioters: Restoring faith in justice. *The Courier*. http://www.thecourier.com.au/story/4660024/theyoungmoom bariotersrestoringfaithinjustice/

Wright, L. (2007, February 4). Lock out these refugee thugs. *Sunday Herald Sun.* https://www.heraldsun.com.au/news/victoria/lock-out-these-refugee-thugs/news-story/f3b4ecd7456cd582ce42d20b78a4e591

Xureb, M., & Evans, C. (2007, October 15). At Highpoint, it's calm after Saturday's storm. *The Age.* http://www.theage.com.au/news/national/at-highpoint-its-calm-after-saturdays-storm/2007/10/14/1192300601244.html

Young, J. (1999). *The exclusive society social exclusion, crime and difference in late modernity.* Sage Publications.

Younge, G. (2018, February 7). Ambalavaner Sivanandan obituary. *The Guardian.* https://www.theguardian.com/world/2018/feb/07/ambalavaner-sivanandan

Yuval-Davis, N. (2006). Belonging and the politics of belonging. *Patterns of Prejudice, 40*(3), 197–214.

Yuval-Davis, N. (2010). Theorizing identity: Beyond the 'us' and 'them' dichotomy. *Patterns of Prejudice, 44*(3), 261–280. https://doi.org/10.1080/0031322X.2010.489736

Yuval-Davis, N. (2011). *The politics of belonging: Intersectional contestations.* Sage.

Zedner, L. (2006). Neither safe nor sound: The perils and possibilities of risk. *Canadian Journal of Criminology and Criminal Justice, 48*(3), 423–434.

Zedner, L. (2009). *Security.* Routledge.

Zedner, L. (2010). Security, the state and the citizen: The changing architecture of crime control. *New Criminal Law Review, 13*(2), 379–403.

Zervos, C., Minear, T., & Alison, G. (2018, January 2). Labor MPs warn voters will punish the Andrews Government if it does not tackle gang crime. *Herald Sun (Australia).* https://www.heraldsun.com.au/news/victoria/labor-mps-warn-voters-will-punish-the-andrews-government-if-it-does-not-tackle-gang-crime/news-story/6e97fb1ef247a6697898cc59b295454f

Zhou, S., Page-Gould, E., Aron, A., Moyer, A., & Hewstone, M. (2019). The extended contact hypothesis: A meta-analysis on 20 years of research. *Personality and Social Psychology Review, 23*(2), 132–160.

Zielinski, C., & Booker, C. (2016, April 11). Moomba riots: Police rule out race as a motive. *The Age.* https://www.theage.com.au/national/victoria/police-charge-24-over-moomba-riots-20160411-go34vr.html

Index

www.ingramcontent.com/pod-product-compliance
Lightning Source LLC
Chambersburg PA
CBHW070347270326
41926CB00017B/4020